DON'T BUY THE LIE
DISCERNING TRUTH IN A WORLD OF DECEPTION

by MARK MATLOCK

DON'T BUY THE LIE
DISCERNING TRUTH IN A WORLD OF DECEPTION

invert
www.invertbooks.com

ZONDERVAN
WWW.ZONDERVAN.COM

by **MARK MATLOCK**

ZONDERVAN

Don't Buy the Lie: Discerning Truth in a World of Deception
Copyright © 2004 by Mark Matlock

Youth Specialties products, 300 South Pierce Street, El Cajon, CA 92020, are
published by Zondervan, 5300 Patterson Avenue SE, Grand Rapids, MI 49530

Library of Congress Cataloging-in-Publication Data

Matlock, Mark.
  Don't buy the lie : discerning truth in a world of deception / by Mark Matlock.
    p. cm.
  ISBN-13: 978-0-310-25814-6
  1. Church work with teenagers. 2. Teenagers—Religious life. 3. Teenagers—
Conduct of life. I. Title.
  BV4447.M343 2004
  261.5'13—dc22
                                                                 2004008617

Editorial direction by Rick Marschall and Doug Davidson
Art direction by Jay Howver
Editing by Doug Davidson
Proofreading by Anita Palmer
Cover design by Burnkit
Interior design by Holly Sharp
Printed in the United States of America

To my children Dax and Skye

The world you are growing up in is so different from my own and yet very similar. You have felt the cost of this book more than any other and my prayer is that you will continue to glorify God in your lives in whatever you may do. Now that this is done ... Let's play. Daddy loves you.

"Don't Buy the Lie" is based on a theme we did for our PlanetWisdom conference. While this book goes well beyond that experience, many people made contributions along the way and I'd like to recognize them. Chris Lyon (who helped extensively on this book), Todd Temple, Mike Gwartney, David McDaniel, Jonathan Matlock, and Don Wayne.

I'd also like to thank Doug Tegner at National Network of Youth Ministers for asking me to do an article on the "thinking traps" that inspired Jay Howver to talk me into expanding the article into a book. I'd also like to recognize Rick Marschall, Roni Meek, and Doug Davidson for their fine editorial contributions.

Solomon wrote that two have a better return on their labor than one, and this wisdom is timeless. Without my wife, Jade, more than half of my work would remain incomplete. This is her journey too, even if she doesn't get as much credit as I do. We are one.

Table of Contents

CHAPTER 1: IN THE DARK

You were just a little kid, but you knew what you had seen. Something had moved in the corner of your room or you'd glimpsed a shape just on the edge of your vision. Maybe you'd heard what sounded like a voice. Was it a monster? A ghost? A "bad guy"?

Afraid to move and call attention to yourself, you lay perfectly still, eyes squeezed not quite shut, hoping whatever it was wouldn't notice you. Finally, you couldn't take it anymore and called for mom and dad to come and investigate—or ran to their room as fast as you could. By the time they got there, though, the thing was always gone. Or hiding...

•••

A friend reads your horoscope to you out of a magazine. You don't really buy all that stuff, but it does seem to fit your personality. The more you think about it, the more it seems like the horoscope was pretty much right in its predictions about your life. You wonder how someone you've never met can write something that matches your life so closely.

•••

A guy on TV gathers a studio audience together like he's going to do another *Oprah*-style talk show. Instead, he says that all these spirits are talking to him. Spirits of the dead. He starts repeating to the audience some of the things that one spirit is telling him, looking for the person who would know this spirit. He tells things from the spirit that only that person could know. The person usually ends up crying because they're so glad to have a message from a loved one who has died. And the message is always so hopeful.

•••

12

You're riding with friends or your family in a car. Suddenly, you realize that you're about to crash. Even though everything feels like it's moving in slow motion, you can't do anything to prevent the accident from happening. Then, at the last possible second, somehow the accident that should have killed or hurt all of you is miraculously avoided. Everyone is fine. You wonder if an angel has just stepped in and saved you.

•••

At a party, someone brings out a Ouija (pronounced "wee-jee") board. As one or two people hold the pointer, you begin asking the board questions about boyfriends, or relatives who have passed away, or what's going to happen in the future. You hear a noise in the other room, and you all jump and laugh. You know it's just a stupid game, but you can't help feeling a little creeped out.

•••

You've learned in Sunday school and church that God's Holy Spirit comes to all who trust in Jesus. And you know you've experienced moments in which you felt God's presence or you sensed a supernatural ability to do something he wanted you to do—like encouraging a friend or telling someone else what you believe.

•••

You laugh when you see a woman on TV telling people what their pets really think about Aunt Millie or the new baby or the Puppy Chow. Still, she seems to know things the people haven't told her. But how could anyone believe a psychic was communicating with pooches and parakeets?

13

•••

A friend or a "friend of a friend" or someone on the Internet tells you that he's part of the Wiccan religion. He says that they worship nature, and that they're learning how to get supernatural power through spells or castings or chanting. Maybe he tells you he's going to become a warlock. You wonder if these people have any kind of power at all. And you wonder what it would be like to have power like that.

•••

A popular TV show features witches, vampires, or demons who save the day—or maybe the world—using their special powers. Although once evil, they now use their darkness to fight against *really* evil stuff. Cartoons, books, and movies you've seen describe good witches and wizards who use magic to do the right thing and stop bad witches and wizards. You wonder if maybe witchcraft has been given a bad name.

•••

A missionary comes to your church and talks about seeing people in a foreign country who were demon-possessed. They talked in strange voices saying awful things and hurting themselves. You remember times when you felt like you were in the presence of some kind of evil, and it made you feel afraid.

•••

You've just watched a scary movie. Maybe it was the story of an evil videotape that causes people to die seven days after they have watched it. And you keep waiting for the TV to turn on by itself and a wicked little girl to climb out and get you. Or maybe the movie focused on a broken family that is living in a haunted house and slowly realizing that they are the ones doing the haunting. Or it could be the tale of a vampire or some other secretly evil creature that makes friends with people and then destroys them when their defenses are down.

Whatever it was, you can't sleep now, and you feel just like you did when you were a little kid. Except now you can't call mom and dad to come and help you look for the monsters. You're pretty sure it's all in your head, but part of you still wonders about all that supernatural stuff.

Are ghosts real? Do angels and demons really work invisibly to help or hurt us? Can some people talk to the dead? Are witches and wizards just for storytelling, or can they be real?

Spiritual = Cool Again

Over the last couple of decades, interest in the spiritual and supernatural has been growing. For most of the twentieth century, "modern" people ignored that world. After all, everything that existed could be explained by science.

The most popular worldview in academics and media was *naturalism*. People who held this view of the world believed that if you could not taste, touch, smell, hear, or see something, it probably didn't exist. All that mattered was what you could experience with your senses. Even people who believed in God didn't have time or interest in "unexplained" phenomenon. Most just considered everything beyond nature and their own religious beliefs to be silly superstition.

15

But the supernatural is back in a big way. As a society, we got frustrated with the limits of what science could tell us about life, including life after death and life's deeper meaning. Today, millions are looking for truth—and power—in the spiritual world. Books, TV shows, and movies about supernatural and spiritual things crowd the tops of the bestseller lists and box office reports.

Since I'm all about talking to teenagers about the supernatural world, I wanted to find out exactly what this generation believes. So I commissioned Barna Research Group to conduct a scientific survey of

Do you believe in a spiritual or supernatural world beyond the range of our senses?

> **WHAT YOUR FRIENDS BELIEVE**

73% Yes   **27% No**

U.S. teenagers. The results surprised me and the rest of my staff. It turns out that nearly three of every four teenagers believe there is, indeed, a world that exists beyond what our senses can detect. As you might guess, however, there's a ton of disagreement about what goes in that world. You'll find the responses of teenagers to various questions on our survey throughout this book—and some of the results may surprise you.

Our survey also told us that people *really* care about this stuff. Part of the attraction is that we want to know what's "out there." We *want* to believe. We're hungry to confirm what our hearts tell us—that power exists beyond what our limited human bodies can experience or produce.

As Bible-believing Christians, we *are* convinced something specific is out there. We know that a supernatural world *does* exist. We believe in an invisible Creator God who raised his own son from the dead and will give us an eternal life after death through that son.

But what about all this other supernatural stuff? What about ghosts and horoscopes and angels and demons and Satan and vampires? How are Christians who take the Bible as God's Word supposed to sort all that out and decide what's true and what's just really creative imagination or—worse—really powerful deception?

That's what this book is all about. We're going to dig into the supernatural world and figure out how to think logically about the unseen. We're going to look at exactly what the Bible teaches about the supernatural. And we're going to pick up a few skills to keep from being deceived by people who lie about supernatural power.

Why does it matter? Because when people go looking for truth in a world of the supernatural, they open themselves up to being deceived. They put themselves right in the crosshairs of the great liar who wants to confuse them about the truth. They're ready to put more value in their "experience" of the supernatural than in the truth behind their experience. I should know. I've spent much of my life using the power of illusion to make it seem as if I had supernatural power.

Art of Deception

My own interest in the supernatural—or at least in *faking* the supernatural—started when I was just a kid. Fascinated by **17** magicians and magic tricks, I spent hours and hours practicing illusions I could show to my friends and family. I loved being able to impress them with my "power." That's why I became a junior member of the prestigious Magic Castle in Southern California at the age of 17. Many famous magicians (as well as folks who work with David Copperfield and David Blaine) belong to this club, along with actors and other celebrities.

Through that association, I met many other illusionists. These men and women could use sleight of hand, diversion, and the power of suggestion to convince people they had powers beyond the natural. As I got older, I made friends who specialized in using "psychic abilities."

> **How much time do you spend thinking about the supernatural world?**
>
> **WHAT YOUR FRIENDS BELIEVE**
>
> | | |
> |---|---|
> | 18% | A lot of time |
> | 36% | Some, but not a lot of time |
> | 47% | Very little or no time |

I was amazed by their ability to convince audiences they could read minds or move objects with their mental energy.

In this group, I got to know two types of illusionists. One group used their skills to entertain audiences—but everyone understood they were being "tricked." The other group of illusionists used their well-practiced abilities to convince people they really could tell the future or read minds or talk to the dead. Either for money or just out of a perverse idea of fun, they would dupe overly trusting people into paying them for information that wasn't real.

In other words, they lied about the supernatural world.

One time, one of these mentalists asked if he could show me something. I sat down across the table from him, and he told me to make a fist with one hand. Then, on a piece of paper, he drew a picture of a hand. Next, he took his cigarette and touched it to the middle of the hand he'd drawn. Of course, the paper caught fire and burned up.

Finally, this guy told me to open my fist. When I did, I found ash right in the spot where he had touched his cigarette to the hand on the paper. Even though I'd been studying illusion for a while, this shocked and startled me. It took me quite a while to figure out exactly how the trick was done—and, yes, it was a trick. But it helped me see how powerful illusion can be in convincing people to believe lies about the supernatural.

Like Fox Mulder on *The X-Files*, people *want* to believe so badly that they'll buy just about anything. They want to experience talking to lost loved ones or knowing the future before it happens. They want to be convinced that the supernatural really

Do you believe that these spiritual beings exist?

> **WHAT YOUR FRIENDS BELIEVE**

Ghosts:
57%   Yes
40%   No
2%   Don't know

Witches:
37%   Yes
63%   No
1%   Don't know

Vampires:
11%   Yes
88%   No
1%   Don't know

exists. So my "psychic friends" gladly took their money and—worse—warped their understanding of reality.

The goal of this book is to help you avoid making the same mistake. Sometimes, it's actually easier to fool Christians about the supernatural because we already believe some supernatural things exist, don't we? We believe in God and Satan and demons and angels. So why not just add ghosts and vampires and talking with the dead to the list? Our supernatural worldview opens us up to deception.

Of course, those with a naturalist view of the world are less likely to get caught believing in supernatural lies. Atheists, agnostics, and pure evolutionists who refuse to believe in any kind of supernatural world are not likely to waste time with spiritual lies. Instead, they'll end up being deceived about what really is true, right? They'll miss out on the true supernatural God and the real supernatural world he controls.

Obviously, it's no good to be deceived about supernatural

things that don't exist. But it's no better to refuse to believe in supernatural things that can save your soul—or put it in danger. We can't just say, "Believe it all." And we certainly can't go back to, "Don't believe any of it." One way or another, we have to figure out what's true and what's a lie when it comes to the supernatural.

We're going to kick this book off with a quick overview of how to think about supernatural stuff. Then we'll dig into exactly what the Bible says (and doesn't say) about God and his angels. We'll look at truths, lies, and strange ideas about Satan, demons, hell, and heaven. Along the way, we'll turn the spotlight of God's Word on ghosts, vampires, talking to the dead, and even a young wizard named Harry.

I hope you're ready to do more than just experience the supernatural. I hope you're ready to let God teach you the truth about what goes on behind the veil of the natural world—what's real, what's fake, and how you can live every day "supernaturally."

CHAPTER 2: THE BEREAN PRINCIPLE

At the same time Barna Research was conducting our nationwide survey of teen beliefs about the supernatural, we were asking visitors to our Web site, PlanetWisdom.com, to tell us about *their* supernatural experiences. We got some wild responses.

One user who claimed to be a former Wiccan and warlock described a moment when he was convinced a ghost had turned on a water facet. Another user told about the time her deceased grandmother visited her in her room. And one female respondent wrote about a day when a guy friend claimed to have been pushed on top of her by an unseen supernatural force when they were alone—and he couldn't get off her for several minutes.

Obviously, people writing to a Web site could say anything. We don't know for sure that these events happened. And that's the point. How do you make up your mind about what's possible and what's clearly wrong about the supernatural? How would you respond if a friend of yours described an experience like one of these? Is there any way to know if such things really happened—or if they're just lies, confusion, or misunderstandings?

The Discernment Muscle

Of course, there's no way to verify for sure what happened while someone was alone. However, we don't have to settle for just wondering what's possible in the supernatural world. The Bible teaches that we can use *discernment* to figure out what's real and what's fake in our lives.

The dictionary defines *discernment* as "keen insight" or "good judgment." The Bible usually uses the word when describing the ability to tell right from wrong or truth from lies. In Deuteronomy 32:28, an entire nation is described as being "without sense" because they don't have the discernment to make good choices about right and wrong or good and evil.

People without discernment are the most likely to believe lies about the supernatural world. They're the ones who either swallow every idea and experience that comes along—or reject God because he can't be experienced with their senses. You and I need discernment to figure out the truth about supernatural things.

Where do you get that kind of discernment? Well, we know from the Bible that God gives discernment, because he gave it to both David and his son Solomon (1 Kings 3:11-12; 2 Chronicles 2:12). So it makes sense to start by asking God to give you the discernment to tell truth from lies about spiritual things. That's what David did (Psalm 119:125).

But discernment is kind of like athletic ability. If you don't use it, you could lose it. If you let your discernment muscle get flabby and start hanging over your belt, it won't be there when you need it most. Job wrote that God can take away the discernment of those who once had it (Job 12:20). And a man of great discernment, Solomon, wrote that you have to work to hold on to it: "Preserve sound judgment and discernment, do not let them out of your sight" (Proverbs 3:21).

But what can you do to build up that discernment muscle? How can you work out to become stronger and stronger in the area of discernment about supernatural things? You have to practice.

During his travels around the world of his day, Paul found a group of people who were excellent at practicing discernment. Listen to what Acts 17:11-12 says about the Christians in the town of Berea:

> Now the Bereans were of more noble character than the Thessalonians, for they received the message with great eagerness and examined the Scriptures every day to see if what Paul said was true. Many of the Jews believed, as did also a number of prominent Greek women and many Greek men.

Did you catch the Bereans' attitude toward new information? First, they were eager—or open-minded—to learn the truth. They weren't closed to ideas they didn't understand. They didn't run from new experiences or concepts that were uncomfortable. They wanted to hear what Paul had to say about God; they wanted to grow in their knowledge of the supernatural.

From that, we learn that practicing discernment starts with listening and learning. What, exactly, does someone want you to believe about the supernatural? What are the details of what your friend experienced? What exactly is that TV show or scary movie suggesting about the world beyond our senses? If you had a strange experience, what can you say happened—for sure? Discernment starts with taking the time to get the facts straight.

Next, the Bereans were *eager* to learn the truth. They didn't stop with the facts; they wanted to understand the meaning *behind* the facts so they could live their lives according to the truth. They didn't settle for making big assumptions about what was being presented to them.

Finally, this muscular group of discerners didn't simply take what Paul said at face value. They didn't just flip around the TV dial of their day drinking in every new idea and accepting it as truth. Instead, they compared everything Paul taught them with the truth of *Scripture* to make sure it was true. The Bereans understood that God's Word was the standard for all truth. If an idea or experience contradicted Scripture, they threw it out as a lie.

What has the greatest influence on your views about the supernatural?

> **WHAT YOUR FRIENDS BELIEVE**

%	Source
31%	Not sure
18%	Family or parents
9%	My faith
8%	My pastor or church
7%	The Bible
10%	My own experiences or perspectives
6%	TV shows and movies
5%	Friends
2%	School or teachers
5%	Other sources

That's practicing discernment. Listen. Understand. Compare with Scripture. Every new bit of info about the supernatural world should go through that filter in your brain. Listen. Understand. Compare with Scripture. That's the pattern of critical thinking for a Christian.

Building Your Filter

Obviously, the Berean Principle won't work if one of the components in your filter breaks down, will it? You can't practice discernment if you don't listen, learn, and compare with Scripture.

Not Listening

Let's start with listening. You'd think that any of us could take the time to listen to what was being presented about the supernatural if we really wanted to discern the truth. But listening is often the last thing on our lists of things to do.

For instance, someone who has already decided there's no way any supernatural force could have been involved in the origin of the world might not take the time to listen to the evidence for an intelligent designer. That person might just tune out immediately when someone starts to talk about creation.

On the other side of the block, closed-minded Christians often miss opportunities to help clear up misunderstandings about the supernatural simply because they don't take the time to listen to those who have questions. Sometimes, we refuse to hear anything about ghosts or psychics or vampires, because we've already made up our minds about them.

But taking the time to listen gives us another chance to help someone (or ourselves) discern the truth about strange or unexplained experiences.

Another reason people don't listen is *fear*. The supernatural world is just so scary for some folks that they don't want to hear anything about it. Or they're afraid that listening to someone talk about communication with the dead or other strange happenings will cause them to doubt their own beliefs.

But fear is a lousy reason for not practicing discernment about spiritual things. The Bible is clear that fear does not come from God (2 Timothy 1:7). God is not only big enough to protect us from the supernatural world, he's big enough to handle any hard questions that comes up when we take the time to listen to what others are saying about spiritual things. If God is really God, hard questions aren't going to shake him—and they don't need to keep us from listening.

Not Understanding

Sometimes, discernment breaks down in the understanding phase. We think we've heard what the person or movie or teacher or experience is saying, but we didn't actually get the meaning straight.

For instance, I use illusions in my teaching to illustrate some of the truths of God's Word. Although I say over and over again in my teaching sessions that I have no magic powers—that everything I do is completely natural, using the techniques of slight of hand, power of suggestion, and lots of practice—some people still think I'm claiming to be magic. They don't want to have anything to do with me, because the illusions cause them to jump to the conclusion that I have demonic power.

Those people hear me just like everyone else in the room does, but they miss the understanding part. Without the understanding, discernment is impossible. Much of what we'll deal with in the second half of this book involves learning to understand what we hear and see.

Another example of not understanding is when we hear just enough to think we already know all about what is being said or shown to us. For instance, some people assume that all religious people believe you can go to heaven if your good deeds outweigh your bad ones. So when they listen long enough to hear that you're a Christian, they respond by saying, "Yeah, I've lived a pretty good life; I think I'll make it to heaven." Then they shut down. They stop you before you can explain the grace of God for all sinners.

They hear our words, but they don't take the next step in discernment that involves really understanding what we believe. Christians often do the same when unbelievers start talking about their supernatural beliefs. We assume we understand without actually taking the time to fully grasp what that other person is trying to tell us. Discernment can't happen without understanding.

Not Comparing with Scripture

For Christians, this is the biggie. We start with the assumption that the Bible is the standard for what's true; it is God's Word to humans. Obviously, those who don't believe in Scripture will disagree with us about the Bible. And that's fine. We don't expect them to hold to the same standard we do.

It's especially important to realize that the phrase "because the Bible says so" doesn't prove anything to non-Christians. It's not evidence for them, and it shouldn't be. We can't use the Bible as an argument to prove our beliefs to others about demons, angels, and God.

However, the Bible's position on an issue makes a huge difference to people who claim to believe it. It makes all the difference to me. And this book is aimed at Bible-believing Christians who want to listen and understand the truth about all the strange supernatural things we hear about in the world today. If you don't believe the Bible is true, you might not agree with a lot of the conclusions we come to. But if you want to better understand what Christians believe about the supernatural, stick around.

For Christians, then, discernment breaks down when we forget to compare what we hear and experience with the truth of God's Word. I'm often shocked by Christian students who claim to believe the Bible is true, but also claim to believe the exact opposite of what the Bible teaches.

For instance, many Christians don't see any problem with cheating on a test, even though they claim to understand that the Bible teaches us not to lie. Others believe a person should definitely seek revenge when he or she is treated badly, even though God clearly tells us not to do that in Scripture. These students (and adults) lack discernment in making decisions because they're not willing or interested in comparing their experience with what the Bible teaches.

The same thing happens with beliefs about the supernatural world. Our study revealed that many teenagers believe in heaven, but not hell; God, but not Satan; and angels, but not demons. These teenagers have decided that they like some parts of the Bible, but not others.

Instead of comparing new ideas against Scripture, they compare it against what makes sense or sounds good *to them*. They've made themselves their own standard for evaluating what is or isn't true about the supernatural. That doesn't lead to biblical discernment. That leads to confused and chaotic thinking. It also leads into dangerous supernatural territory.

> **Do you believe that good and evil exist in the supernatural world?**
>
> **WHAT YOUR FRIENDS BELIEVE**
>
> 59% Yes
> 38% No
> 3%   Don't know

Of course, just believing the Bible is true doesn't automatically make you an expert in what Scripture teaches. In order to flex our discernment muscles like the *Bereans* about supernatural stuff, we have to learn exactly what the Bible says about angels, demons, heaven, hell, God, Satan, and all the other "beyond natural" issues we confront. The next few chapters will help us dig deep enough into God's Word to become well-equipped discerners.

CHAPTER 3: THE ULTIMATE SUPERNATURAL BEING

Does God exist? That's the biggest supernatural question of all, isn't it? If there is a God, he'd be the ultimate supernatural being. Invisible. Undetectable with our senses. Everywhere at once. The power to control everything.

When you think about it, the idea of God can be pretty scary. An all-powerful being who knows everything—including your thoughts and feelings. Someone "out there" who can control nature, people, the future. Beyond that, this ultimate spirit would even have the power to decide what happens to you and the people you love after you die.

That's some serious power. But what does God have to do with all the other spiritual ideas and supernatural worldviews popping up in our culture right now? If God is real, why don't we hear more about such a powerful force?

Usually, movies and TV shows that deal with the supernatural create worlds that are completely godless. In *The Ring,* for example, ghosts and evil exist with no mention of God. And Nicole Kidman's *The Others* showed a woman who believed in a very harsh God that turned out to have no influence on the afterlife, after all. Horror movies are notorious for focusing completely on the power of supernatural evil without a peep about God.

Television shows like *Buffy the Vampire Slayer*, *Angel*, and *Charmed* dismiss the idea of a single supernatural God for a universe filled with many gods and/or veiled references to "the powers that be." It's especially strange in the worlds of *Buffy* and *Angel* because these shows deal with religious things like demons and crosses and holy water. They give power to the symbols that represent an idea of God while almost exclusively ignoring him.

What is God like?

WHAT YOUR FRIENDS BELIEVE

71%	The all-powerful, all-knowing, perfect creator of the world who rules the world today
9%	Represents the state of higher consciousness that a person may reach
5%	Refers to the realization of total human potential
4%	Everyone is God
4%	There are many gods, each with different power and authority
7%	Other/don't know

One exception is the recent hit TV show *Joan of Arcadia*. The creators of that show not only embrace a somewhat traditional idea of God, they show him appearing to Joan and using her to accomplish his will on earth and in the lives of her friends and family.

So what about the "real" God? Does God exist? Does God care about us? Does God want anything from us? Your answers to those questions say a lot about your view of the spiritual world.

Worldview Matters

32 What you believe about the existence of God is step one in deciding your *worldview*. Your worldview is the collection of things you believe to be true about life and the way things work. In a way, it's like the filter we talked about in the last chapter. Every piece of information you experience is viewed through the lens of your worldview.

For instance, if you're a boy-crazy girl whose worldview is that Orlando Bloom is the hottest guy on the planet, you'll pay attention to every magazine cover with his picture on it. You'll talk about him with your friends. You'll stare longingly at paused images of him on your *Pirates of the Caribbean* DVD.

But if you're a grandmother who thinks Orlando Bloom sounds like a rare flower from Florida, you probably wouldn't even notice the magazines or care if someone suggests that another actor is hotter. Your worldview changes how you see the world.

Silly example for a serious point. Why should we care about worldview? Because of this formula: Worldview defines beliefs. Beliefs define values. Values define behavior.

Whether we ever think about it or not, our worldview determines what decisions we'll make in life.

For instance, let's start with the two biggest categories of worldview—belief in a supernatural God (*theism*) or belief in no God at all (*atheism*). Notice that I called them both beliefs. Neither can be proven completely. Both worldview positions must be arrived at by making a choice after looking at limited evidence. Both require faith.

So let's say you've decided to believe God does *not* exist. That's your worldview. If God does not exist, what will you believe about the origin of human life? It must have come into being by chance, right? Humans are just animals who happen to have benefited from millions of years of evolution.

33

How does your belief about the origin of life affect the value you place on human life? Well, if we're all just accidents, how valuable can we be? The "laws" of evolution demand that the weakest and least productive do not survive, right?

And how does that low value on human life shape our decisions? If human life is not all that special—if we believe in survival of the fittest—then stealing, abortion, murder, and other acts of cruelty to each other might be justifiable choices. Our godless worldview leaves the door open to treating other humans as disposable.

On the other hand, a worldview that includes God would lead to a belief that humans are his creation, which should lead us to put a high value on human life. So our decisions in life would be made in a way that treats each human being with compassion.

Sounds like we'd better be pretty clear on exactly what we believe about the existence of God—and what he's like if he's really "out there."

Is God?

Remember, our big survey revealed that 27 percent of teenagers believe there is no spiritual world at all. That would include God. The lens through which these atheists look at the world does not allow for the possibility that God is real nor that he has any influence on their world.

34   That's a lot of your peers who have decided to live their lives according to the idea that we are alone on earth with what our senses can reveal. On the other hand, most teenagers—and most Americans of any age—do believe in a supernatural being called God, who is the "all-powerful, all-knowing, perfect creator of the universe who rules the world today." In fact, 75 percent of students who believe in a real supernatural world have that idea of God.

Can we know for sure that God exists? Nope. That is, we can't offer complete and irrefutable evidence of God's existence that humans can experience with their senses. We can't measure God or weigh him or use night-vision goggles to pick up his body heat. By definition, God is supernatural. He's beyond our senses.

But does believing in God make sense for reasonable people if they are willing to look at the evidence? Yup. We don't have room in this book to lay out all the logical arguments for the existence of God (check out Lee Strobel's *The Case for Faith*, if you really want to dig into it). But everything from the complexity and beauty of our universe to the human tendency to believe in right and wrong to the extreme reliability of the Bible points to a massively intelligent designer running the show somewhere.

Just the fact that so many people from so many walks of life believe in God is evidence that we come "pre-installed" with the idea that God is. To reject belief in God, we have to go against our programming. The biblical author Paul wrote this:

> ...what may be known about God is plain to them, because God has made it plain to them. For since the creation of the world God's invisible qualities—his eternal power and divine nature—have been clearly seen, being understood from what has been made, so that men are without excuse. (Romans 1:19-20)

Rejecting God because we can't see, touch, or taste him in person is "no excuse." In fact, Paul suggests you really have to work to throw off your natural tendency to believe in God. You have to *want* him not to exist. King David even wrote, "The fool says in his heart, 'There is no God'" (Psalm 14:1).

Whether six million American teenagers believe it or not, God is "out there." But what is he like? And what, exactly, is he doing?

Being God

Again, the idea of an all-power supernatural being who likes to get involved with humans could be the scariest horror movie ever. Or it could be the greatest hope that humanity has known. It all depends on what that supernatural God is like—and how we respond to him.

As Christians, we believe the Bible tells us a ton about who God is and what he does. He's not easy to understand, but let's dig into a few things we can know about this supernatural wonder.

One All-Powerful Creator God

As God's people have said since ancient times about this eternal spiritual being, "The LORD our God, the LORD is one" (Deuteronomy 6:4).

The Bible is clear that there is no battle in the heavens among many gods for control of the universe. Unlike the worlds pictured in *Hercules, Xena* and *Charmed,* we believe in one God who alone created and controls everything in the universe (Genesis 1; Ephesians 1; Revelation 19:6).

Yes, this God has three distinct persons—the Father, the Son, and the Holy Spirit—but mysteriously he is still one God.

All-Knowing Holy Unchanging Everywhere God

Not only does God have power over everything, he knows everything (1 John 3:20) and he is everywhere at the same time (Psalm 139:7-12). That means we are never "away" from God, and he is never unaware of what's going on in our hearts, minds, and lives.

If that weren't enough—and it's a lot—this God is pure God all the time. Another word for that is *holy* (Isaiah 5:16; 1 John 1:5). That's more than just perfect. It's like a bar of the purest gold. There's nothing but gold in there. Since God has always been, he's

God all the way through. Nothing else defines him.

And God is always who he was and who he will be (James 1:17). That, at least, tells us that his character is somewhat predictable. We don't have to worry that he will change all the laws of the universe tomorrow. He does what he says. Always.

So far, we've got the most powerful supernatural being anyone could imagine. We've defined a lot of power and ability. But what does God do with all that control?

God Works Out His Plan

I don't know the details of God's full plan for the world or for my life. But the Bible teaches that he knows and that he's in full control. Yes, that's hard to understand when the worst happens and pain lingers. But God is God. By definition, he's running the show and moving humanity toward the future that he has designed (Romans 8:28).

The Jim Carrey comedy *Bruce Almighty* could be accused of belittling God in some ways. However, the filmmakers did a surprisingly good job of showing that only God can be God. After trying out God's powers for a few days, Bruce finally breaks down and admits he was wrong to blame God for all his troubles. He actually repents to God for his pride and agrees to trust God with his life—right there in a big Hollywood movie.

God Tells the Truth

Hebrews 6:18 says that God cannot lie, and God's Son Jesus defined himself as "truth." That means God will never use his supernatural power and control to deceive us. That's just not in God. And for those of us who believe the Bible is his Word, we can trust every verse of it to be truth.

God Loves

More specifically, God *is* love (1 John 4:8). By definition God loves everyone. I know people question this because of all the suffering in the world, but God loved everyone in the world so much that he gave his own Son to pay for the sin that causes all that suffering (John 3:16).

38   To get more personal (and more mind-blowing), this ultimate supernatural being loves you and he loves me. He loved us enough to let his own Son die so we could live forever.

God Provides One Way

God has established that the *only* way to be with him forever is to trust in his Son Jesus for our place in God's family. We cannot get there on our own because we are all sinners (Romans 3:23). God's supernatural *and* human Son Jesus said, "I am the way and the truth and the life. No one comes to the Father except through me" (John 14:6).

Many "spiritual" people will tell you that this view of God is intolerant and narrow-minded. What about all the other spiritual paths out there? At least, they say, we should allow for the possibility of supernatural things beyond our knowing. Even the God-oriented *Bruce Almighty* and *Joan of Arcadia* carefully avoid suggesting that Jesus is the only way to the Father.

But the Bible's point is that sin must be paid for, and that Jesus paid for it with his blood. What other path could there be to Jesus' Father except through Jesus? (Hebrews 9:22)

God Provides Justice

Those who reject God by rejecting his Son will pay for their sin forever in hell. With all his supernatural power and love, God will allow them to have a Godless, torment-filled eternity apart from him (2 Thessalonians 1:8-9).

God Provides His Spirit

39

Talk about supernatural! This member of the Trinity (the three persons that make up our one God) used to be called the Holy Ghost, but he's not a ghost in the sense of a dead person lingering on earth. Instead, he's the very essence of who God is.

The amazing thing is that this Holy Spirit is given to all who trust in Christ for salvation. This gift of the Holy Spirit is a promise that we belong to God (Ephesians 1:13). With God's Spirit, Christians are capable of amazing supernatural things. We'll find out more about that later in the book.

Knowing God

Does this God sound different than the one who shows up (or doesn't) in TV shows, books, and movies that deal with the supernatural world? How does the God of the Bible compare with other ideas of him?

Stop me if you've heard these: "God represents the state

of higher consciousness that a person may reach." "There are many gods, each with different power and authority." "God refers to the realization of total human potential." And the real doozy: "We're all gods or part of the larger idea of god."

These are beliefs offered every day in entertainment, philosophy classes, and sometimes even in churches. If you're a Christian, getting to know the true, biblical God will give you the power to spot these lies about the supernatural being who will definitely have the biggest impact on your life. In fact, God is the first and most important spiritual entity you need to worry about. As we'll see in coming chapters, all other supernatural beings are under his control.

Right now, let's separate the myth from the fantasy about one of the most misunderstood spiritual beings in the universe—angels.

CHAPTER 4: THE TRUTH
ABOUT ANGELS

Things looked grim to Elisha's servant. He and Elisha were staying in the city of Dotham in Israel, and they were suddenly in big trouble. After rolling off his mat one morning and stepping outside, the servant saw that the small city was surrounded by a strong force of enemy soldiers who had moved their horses and chariots quietly into position during the night (2 Kings 6:15).

The servant knew that danger was part of Elisha's job description. As God's prophet on earth, Elisha received supernatural messages from God that he delivered to God's people. This often got him in trouble.

Just recently, God had been telling Elisha where the enemy Aramean army was planning raids on Israel. Elisha kept passing the info on to the king of Israel, who was then able to guard against the raids each time.

This really ticked off the king of Aram. Convinced he had a traitor in his camp leaking intelligence to the Israelites, he called his officers together to figure out who it was. But one officer knew the whole deal about Elisha and told the king that the prophet Elisha supernaturally knew everything the king planned—even when the king was alone in his bedroom!

Not thinking too far ahead, the king made a new plan—get Elisha! He sent a strong force to Dotham to capture the prophet, apparently not considering that Elisha would know he was coming.

But if Elisha did know, he didn't let on to his servant, who now saw a whole lot of enemy spears and horse hooves between him and safety. The servant was scared.

Elisha was not. He told his servant this: "Don't be afraid. Those who are with us are more than those who are with them" (2 Kings 6:16). That must have been confusing, since the servant could only see himself, Elisha, and a bunch of soldiers wearing the other team's colors.

Then Elisha asked the most powerful supernatural force in the universe to let his servant see beyond the natural world to the supernatural. When he turned around, the servant suddenly saw the hills around Dotham full of "chariots of fire" and horses that easily outnumbered the enemy forces.

Elisha's servant realized it wasn't he who was doomed—it was the Arameans. God's supernatural army was protecting Elisha from the suddenly flimsy-looking Aramean force. You can read the rest of this exciting story in 2 Kings 6.

The passage doesn't say specifically that the supernatural fiery chariots seen by Elisha's servant were led by angels, but that would make sense. The point is that there's a whole supernatural world out there we never see or know about. God uses these usually invisible forces to accomplish his will on earth.

Let's find out more about these supernatural servants of God.

Misunderstanding Angels

In *City of Angels*, Nicolas Cage plays an angel who falls in love with a mortal woman and chooses to become mortal himself. In *Michael*, John Travolta is an irresponsible angel who smokes, eats too much sugar, and generally behaves badly. In countless other films, angels are shown helping humans fall in love or see the value of their lives (*It's a Wonderful Life*) or even win baseball games (*Angels in the Outfield*).

43

In classic art, angels are pictured as everything from chubby babies with wings to beautiful floating women in long gowns to

Do you believe that angels exist?	
WHAT YOUR FRIENDS BELIEVE	
89%	Yes
10%	No
1%	Don't know

powerfully muscled, winged men. In newspaper and magazine stories, angels are regularly given credit for stepping in at the last minute to save lives supernaturally.

In the greeting card section at your supermarket, baby cards welcome the birth of little angels while sympathy cards suggest that your departed loved one has become an angel. Parents everywhere hope desperately that each child has a guardian angel—something nearly 80 percent of the teenagers in our survey believe. In fact, angels are the one spiritual being that most people believe in.

Over the last few years, interest in angels has skyrocketed. A quick search on the Internet will reveal angel magazines, books, movies, and music—not to mention angel jewelry, clothing lines, and artwork.

As humans, the idea that there are unseen angels among us, working to make sure everything turns out okay, is powerful and hopeful. But because people want to believe in angels, many will believe almost anything about them. Christians, Wiccans, and even some atheists claim to believe in angels—but obviously they don't all agree on what those angels are like.

44 So how can we sort out the truth about angels from all the other ideas out there? Are angels really former humans? Can they sin or make mistakes? Are they always watching us? What powers do they have?

As always, we believe that God's Word is the standard for truth. So everything we can know for sure about angels, we'll find in there. And there's plenty to find. Angels are mentioned 108 times in the Old Testament and 165 times in the New Testament. Let's dig in.

Where Do Angels Come From?

The book of Job describes a group of spiritual beings that many scholars assume to be angels. These beings existed before the earth was created (Job 38:6-7). And we know they were specially created by God, because in Colossians 1:16-17, Paul explains that God created every kind of being: "For by him all things were created: things in heaven and on earth, visible and invisible, whether thrones or powers or rulers or authorities; all things were created by him and for him."

We know angels are not former (or glorified) humans based on several passages. Some people get confused because of Jesus' statement that at the resurrection, we will be "like the angels in heaven" (Matthew 22:30). But the first half of that sentence is that we will not marry in heaven—just as the angels don't marry.

To make it even clearer, a description of heaven in the book of Hebrews lists both the "spirits of righteous men made perfect" *and* "thousands upon thousands of angels" (Hebrews 12:22-23). Angels and humans are different groups in the city of God.

Angles are not a race, like humanity. The Bible never speaks of "sons of angels." Apparently, angels never have little angels. And Jesus said that angels don't die, either (Luke 20:36). God's Word seems to teach that all angels were created at the same time and will exist forever.

45

And God must have created a lot of them, because Daniel 7:10 describes the throne room of God with what seems to be millions of angels. Jesus claimed that the Father could send tens of thousands of angels to him (Matthew 26:53), and Hebrews 12:22 paints the picture of "thousands upon thousands" of angels in the city of God.

What Do Angels Look Like?

Remember, angels are supernatural beings that are usually invisible to humans. So most of the time, they don't look like anything—at least to us. Described as "ministering spirits" (Hebrews 1:14), angels don't require a physical body at all. They exist in the spiritual world beyond our senses.

However, the Bible includes many stories of times when angels appeared to humans, so we know they can reveal themselves to us when they need to. In Scripture, angels take several different forms.

Most often, angels appear to people in human form, as three did when they delivered a birth announcement to Abraham (Genesis 18-19). And many folks are surprised to realize that, in those few cases where an angel's gender is specified in the Bible, the angel is always a full-grown man—never a chubby baby, and never, strangely, is a biblical angel specifically depicted as female. So the painters and storytellers who create feminine and baby angels have great imaginations, but their angel pictures aren't based on Scripture.

God's Word also includes several stories about times when angels appeared much more "angel-like"—in long, white robes (Mark 16:5) or with a dazzling, bright light (Luke 2:9) or flying with wings (Isaiah 6:2). And often, an angel who appears to humans must start by saying, "Don't be afraid!" From that, we can guess that angels can look intimidating when not "disguised" as normal looking people.

The descriptions of some angels are just plain strange to us. The *seraphs* or *seraphim* that Isaiah saw are described as having six wings and using two to cover their feet, two to cover their faces, and two to fly.

The descriptions of the *cherubim*, another type of angel (we don't know how many types exist), get even stranger. In chapter 10 of his book, Ezekiel pictured these angels as having four faces (human, ox, lion, and eagle), along with hands and wings. They're also presented, among other things, as being covered with eyes and being wheels within wheels. What strange and wonderful creatures they must be.

What Powers Do Angels Have?

The short answer is that angels have the power to do anything God asks them to do. However, they're still limited. Angels are created spirit beings, but they're not gods!

We know from numerous passages in the Bible that angels have to travel from place to place—so they can't be everywhere at once. Jesus said that the angels don't know the timing of the end of the world (Matthew 24:36), and Peter wrote that angels "long" to look into certain things (1 Peter 1:12), so we can be sure that angels are not all-knowing. They have limited knowledge.

However, angels do have power to travel from heaven to earth. They have the power to communicate with humans across the supernatural barrier. In 2 Samuel 14:20, angels are described as being wise and knowing much about what happens on the earth. And we know that angels are "mighty" (Psalm 103:20) and "stronger and more powerful" than humans (2 Peter 2:11).

From the stories in the Book of Daniel about angels protecting Daniel from the lions (chapter six) and his friends from the fire (chapter three), we also know that angels can control our natural world with their supernatural power when God directs them to do so.

In other words, angels have the power to do incredible supernatural things on earth and in the world of humans.

The world *angel* comes from the Greek word *aggelos*; it

means "messenger." The angels' number one job, then, is to do deliver God's message, to do God's work. Some religions teach that angels can be called on—used, manipulated—to do what humans tell them to. That's a lie. Angels do the work of God. Period. That's what he created them to do.

Worship God

Within that higher priority, God gives angels many different types of jobs. First and above all in Scripture, angels are shown worshipping and praising God in heaven. In the Book of Isaiah, the seraphs were crying out to one another in voices that shook the room: "Holy, holy, holy is the Lord Almighty; the whole earth is full of his glory" (Isaiah 6:3).

And the millions upon millions of angels in the throne room of God pictured in John's Revelation sing out together in what must be a deafening and awesome chorus: "Worthy is the Lamb, who was slain, to receive power and wealth and wisdom and strength and honor and glory and praise!" (Revelation 5:12)

In eternity, Christians will join that angel chorus, worshipping the Lamb, Jesus Christ, forever.

Help and Serve Christians

Hebrews 1:14 says, "Are not all angels ministering spirits sent to serve those who will inherit salvation?" God uses these mysterious beings to care for his children. Talk about a mystery! How, exactly, do angels get involved in serving believers?

We don't know all that they do for sure. In the Bible,

such angelic service included protecting people from harm as well as breaking them out of jail. We can assume that protecting and delivering are still part of what God uses angels to do in the lives of believers.

Many people have told strange stories of the sudden appearance of a powerful, protective figure at the exact moment of a crisis. They walk away unscratched from an accident that should have killed them. They're suddenly joined in a threatening situation by a group of strong and friendly-looking guys. A kindly stranger tells them exactly the words they need to hear to keep going—and then disappears.

49

Are these angel stories real? Some have been proven false. Others turn out to have rational explanations. But many accounts of such supernatural phenomena remain unsolved. What we know for sure is that God is able to use these supernatural creatures to serve Christians in our moments of need.

One of the great mysteries of the Christian life is that we'll never know on earth exactly what God has done through his angels to keep us safe, to encourage us, to protect us, to prod us on to do his will. It's essential to remember, though, that God is the one who does it. Angels are merely his servants, obeying him by ministering to us.

Interact with Humans Undetected

Part of the reason we don't know how much angels do in our visible world is that they are apparently able to walk among us undetected. Again, the writer of Hebrews says, "Do not forget to entertain strangers, for by so doing some people have entertained angels without knowing it" (13:2).

It's possible that many of us—even you—have had contact with angels disguised in human form.

Are Used to Help Answer Prayer

In Acts 12, God used an angel to answer the prayer of Peter's friends to break Peter out of jail. God can still use angels to answer the prayers of his people. Again, though, we must always remember that it's God answering the prayer and not the angel.

Observe Christians

50   In his New Testament writings, Paul made several references to the fact that angels were aware of and watching believers (1 Corinthians 4:9; 1 Timothy 5:21). And Jesus said the angels in heaven rejoice over one repentant sinner (Luke 15:10).

Obviously, invisible angels are paying attention to our lives, watching us as we grow in our relationship with God through Jesus. The Bible doesn't say that these angels judge us or condemn us. They don't have that authority, and their job is to serve us. But we know that they're watching.

Care for Christians at Death

Probably one of the most comforting thoughts about angels—and one that shows up often in movies and TV shows—is the idea that they help Christ's followers make the transition from this life to the next one.

We get this picture from the story Jesus told about the rich man and a beggar named Lazarus. When Lazarus dies, he is carried by angels to the next life (Luke 16:22).

Deliver God's Instructions

One of the three named angels in the Bible, Gabriel, is specifically identified as the Lord's messenger. He flew in to deliver messages and prophecies from God to Daniel (Daniel 8-9). And he's the "FedEx angel" in the first chapter of Luke who let both Zechariah and Mary know that they were to become parents to miraculous babies. Gabriel or other angels also delivered messages from God to Joseph (Matthew 1:20-21), the women at Jesus' tomb (Luke 24:4-8), and Philip and Cornelius (Acts (8:26; 10:1-8).

51

Does God still use angels to deliver important messages today? We know he can. However, since his Word to us through the Bible is a complete message from him, he might not choose to do it as often.

Battle God's Enemy

The other two angels named in the Bible are Lucifer and Michael. Lucifer, of course, is better known as Satan, the supernatural and powerful enemy of God. Michael is called the Archangel. He apparently commands the "host" or armies of God's angels.

Several times in Scripture, Michael is described as doing battle with Satan and his demonic forces. In Daniel 10, he takes over a battle, so Gabriel can get away to deliver God's message to Daniel. Jude mentions Michael disputing with Satan over the body of Moses. And Revelation 12:7 depicts the first battle, in which Satan ("the dragon") and his forces are cast out of heaven. (More on that in the next chapter.)

How Should We Deal with Angels?

When you really think about it, angels are mind-blowing supernatural creatures. It's no wonder people can't get enough of them. Who wouldn't want to know more about spirit beings who get involved in the lives of humans?

However, God's Word never tells us to make angels a priority in our lives. He doesn't teach us to look for them or have relationships with them. God wants us to know about them, but he wants our attention focused on him. So what *should* we do about angels?

52

Thank God for Angels

What an amazing thing to know that God's angels are always watching us, actively protecting us, ready to serve us in any way that God commands. It is comforting to know that God cares about us that much.

Be Motivated to Live Right

As mentioned before, the angels are watching God's children. The passage in Hebrews 13 encourages Christians to obey God by offering hospitality to strangers because those strangers might be angels. The point wasn't that we should try to "entertain angels," the point is that we should live right because the angels are aware of our actions.

Knowing that angels can see what's happening in our lives can be a kind of accountability—a motivation to do the right thing even when we think nobody is watching us.

THE TRUTH ABOUT ANGELS

Note: That's not something to fear. The angels aren't going to get you. They're not going to report you to God or take away his forgiveness. He already knows everything you do, anyway. In a way, it could be encouraging to know that someone is observing God's lifelong transformation of us into people who live like Jesus.

Don't Worship Angels or Put Too Much Emphasis on Them!

This one is huge—and it's one way our culture can use something good to lead us into areas that are very, very bad.

53

The Greek and Roman culture that surrounded early Christianity was also very "spiritual." Spirit worship and witchcraft and casting spells and calling on gods and spirits and angels to do human bidding were all very popular. Some Christians got caught up in the worship of angels as part of their Christianity, incorrectly believing that angels were just Christian spirits available to use for personal power. They were more excited about the idea of "experiencing" angels than they were about living in Christ.

Paul warned Christians to avoid such people:

Do not let anyone who delights in false humility and the worship of angels disqualify you for the prize. Such a person goes into great detail about what he has seen, and his unspiritual mind puffs him up with idle notions. He has lost connection with the Head, from whom the whole body, supported and held together by its ligaments and sinews, grows as God causes it to grow. (Colossians 2:18-19)

Why is making too big of a deal out of angels such a concern for Christians? Because this is an area in which Christians can be deceived. Either through hoaxes or through a desire to have a supernatural experience, some Christians have been drawn into believing serious lies about God and the supernatural world.

Whether an experience involved an angel or not doesn't really matter in the end. What matters is that God loves us and cares for us—and that he controls what his angels do in our lives. Our relationship with him is through Jesus, not through angels.

The popular show *Touched by an Angel* depicted a group of angels doing God's will by helping people on earth. Many Christians loved that show because it was so positive and talked about God and emphasized the importance of making right choices. But how much did it talk about Jesus? And if a show about angels gives people the idea that they can get to heaven with the help of some wonderful angels but without Jesus, is it doing more harm than good?

In fact, any show, song, movie, or book suggesting that we can get power from God's angels without Jesus is a great big lie. Jesus is our power source. He's our way to the Father. He's our savior.

Some Wiccans love angels. One site I found on the Internet explained how you could pray to angels or set up alters to them or call on them to help you. But people who don't understand the truth about God's angels are opening themselves up to being deceived by a fallen angel called Satan and his army of fallen angels called demons.

In the next chapter, we'll see how Satan uses angel

worship and other supernatural experiences to lead people away from the truth about Jesus.

CHAPTER 5: LIES FROM THE DARKNESS

It's amazing to me how many people I meet who are willing to accept the idea of God and angels but can't quite bring themselves to believe in Satan or demons. Especially in this new "spiritual" age, people seem even less willing to accept that there's a dark side to the supernatural world.

Our survey of American teenagers found that somewhere between 40 and 60 percent believe Satan is a real spiritual entity. That wide margin comes from separate answers to two different questions, and it tells us that a lot of people haven't made up their mind about the devil.

When asked about the reality of demons, 55 percent of the teenagers surveyed said they believed such supernatural creatures are real. But only 26 percent were "very confident." That's almost three of every four teenagers who can't say for sure that evil supernatural beings are at work in the world.

And that's exactly the way Satan wants it. The biblical Satan has a much better chance of accomplishing his mission if most people think he and his army of demons are a myth. Let them think of him as a "symbolic term that people use to describe evil" (21 percent in our survey) or a name that just "represents the state of conflict between good and evil" (17 percent).

If Satan is real—and if he has a purpose in the lives of humans—wouldn't he prefer that most people put him in the same box with mythical monsters like vampires, ghosts, and the wolf man? He'd love us to think we can just forget about him like all the fictional villains who come and go from our TV screens and movie theaters.

For all our scary ideas about the "prince of darkness," the Bible teaches that Satan's greatest weapon is deception. Jesus called him the "father of lies" (John 8:44). As spiritually powerful as he is, he'd much rather confuse you about the truth than make your skin crawl in the darkness.

What is Satan like?

WHAT YOUR FRIENDS BELIEVE

58%	A real spiritual being and the enemy of God
21%	Not a real being, but represents the conflict between good and evil
17%	A symbolic term that people use to describe evil
4%	Other/don't know

Exploring what the Bible has to say about the real Satan starts with understanding that he wasn't always evil.

Wise and Beautiful

In the last chapter, we saw that the Bible only mentions by name three of the millions of angels that exist. One was Gabriel, the herald (or messenger) angel. Another was the archangel Michael, God's warrior. And the final one was Lucifer, the name originally given to perhaps the greatest angel of all—the angel who became Satan.

Our clearest picture of Satan's origin comes from Ezekiel 28:12-19. The chapter begins with Ezekiel's prophesy about the "ruler" of Tyre, a city that was going to be judged by God for rejecting him. That ruler's greatest sin was pride.

Yet at verse 12, the writer shifts focus to the "king of Tyre" and, apparently, begins to describe the fate of a being who was influencing the human ruler of Tyre. They both share the sin of pride, but the supernatural being described in verses 12-19 was not an earthly king. Here's what it says:

> You were the model of perfection, full of wisdom and perfect in beauty. You were in Eden, the garden of God; every precious stone adorned you: ruby, topaz and emerald, chrysolite, onyx and jasper, sapphire, turquoise and beryl. Your settings and mountings were made of gold; on the day you were created they were prepared. (28:12-13)

The fact that this being was in the Garden of Eden is one reason many scholars believe the passage refers to Satan. The ruler of Tyre could not have been in Eden, but we know for sure that "the serpent" was there (Genesis 3).

58

The first thing we notice is that the amazing supernatural creature described here, Satan, started out as a perfect, wise, and beautiful angel of God. Special attention was given to his appearance, and he was dressed in nine of the 12 gemstones that are often listed as being precious to God. He would have been awesome looking.

It's also important to see that, like all the other angels described in the last chapter, Lucifer was a creation. He existed before humans were created, but he has not always existed. At some point, God *made* him.

Movie series like *Star Wars* and *Harry Potter* and other stories based on the worldview of Eastern religions like to picture the supernatural world as a "force" or energy with two halves. One side is good or positive, and the other side is evil or negative.

Thus, the Jedi and the Sith both use the same "force" to battle each other. And the young wizard Harry taps into white or good magic to take on the black magic of his enemies. In this worldview, good and evil balance each other out in the grand scheme of things. They're two sides of the same supernatural coin.

That's not what the Bible teaches. Satan is not the "dark side" of God's power. He doesn't exist to balance the goodness of God. He was created as a good being by a good God.

You were anointed as a guardian cherub, for so I ordained you. You were on the holy mount of God; you walked among the fiery stones. You were blameless in your ways from the day you were created till wickedness was found in you. (28:14-15)

Satan's job was to be a guardian in the mountain of God. We don't know exactly what that means, but it's clear he had great responsibility. He had access to God. And he did his job flawlessly—until his focus shifted from God to himself.

Through your widespread trade you were filled with violence, and you sinned.

So I drove you in disgrace from the mount of God, and I expelled you, O guardian cherub, from among the fiery stones. Your heart became proud on account of your beauty, and you corrupted your wisdom because of your splendor. (28:16-17)

Satan's downfall was that he started to look at everything he had going for him, and he decided he didn't need God. Because of his wealth, power, and beauty, he started thinking he was better than the One who made him and gave him great wealth, power, and beauty. God couldn't allow such arrogance to remain in his presence.

So I threw you to the earth; I made a spectacle of you before kings. By your many sins and dishonest trade you have desecrated your sanctuaries. So I made a fire come out from you, and it consumed you, and I reduced you to ashes on the ground in the sight of all who were watching. All the nations who knew you are appalled at you; you have come to a horrible end and will be no more. (28:17-19)

This prophesy about Satan isn't completely fulfilled yet. Obviously, he's still at work in the world—along with many angels who followed him in his rebellion against God and were cast out of heaven with him (Revelation 12:7-9). We'll see later what his ultimate end will be.

For now, it's important that we realize how beautiful and perfect Satan was before his pride took over. He was designed to bring glory to God. Instead, he wanted glory for himself.

Modern horror and science fiction stories echo the fall of Satan, but with a perverted twist. Mary Shelley's *Frankenstein* tells the story of a creature that becomes stronger than his creator. Likewise, *The Matrix* trilogy is about machines created by humans that eventually take over from the humans and rule them. In the original story, though, the Creator never loses control or power. The creation is never greater than the Creator.

61

What a tragic supernatural story is Lucifer's. And what tragic consequences it has caused in the lives of humans living in the natural world.

Satan's History

Satan, in the form of a serpent, shows up right at the beginning of human history, using his greatest weapon against the brand new humans for the first time. There, in the Garden of Eden, he told his first lie to humans, which Adam and Eve followed into their first sin, for which we all lost paradise and found death (Genesis 3).

From that point on, Satan's mission on earth has been clear. He's here to try to derail God's plan and to "steal and kill and destroy" (John 10:10). Unlike the popular myth, Satan doesn't yet live in hell, waiting for damned souls to show up for torment. He roams the earth, looking to destroy people's lives (1 Peter 5:8).

Satan is mentioned in seven books of the Old Testament, including Job. There, he urges God to let him destroy Job's life in a vain attempt to get Job to curse God (Job 1–2). Job suffers terribly but never gives in.

Satan and his crew of fallen angels are mentioned in nearly every New Testament book, including the Gospels, where he actively works to interfere in God's plan to save humanity through Jesus. Not only does he tempt Jesus to sin after the Christ has been fasting for 40 days, he also later possesses Judas and uses him to betray Jesus. Again, Satan's plan is foiled, and he is defeated once and for all when Jesus succeeds in his mission.

The rest of the New Testament makes clear that Satan is still at work in the lives of humans. Remember, though, he's not a god. He doesn't have any more powers than an angel has. That means he can't be more than one place at a time and he doesn't know everything. Thus, he relies on his well-organized army of demons to kill, steal, and destroy.

Against Non-Christians

Those who have rejected Christ or haven't yet trusted in him for salvation are wide open to the attacks of this supernatural enemy of humanity. And he wants to keep it that way.

Jesus said that the devil "takes away the word from their hearts, so that they may not believe and be saved" (Luke 8:12). And Paul wrote that he "has blinded the minds of unbelievers, so that they cannot see the light of the gospel of the glory of Christ, who is the image of God" (2 Corinthians 4:4).

Maybe you've experienced this with people who just

can't seem to see the truth about Jesus. It's like something else is at work in their hearts, keeping them from getting over the obstacles of unbelief.

Beyond that, the other fallen angels in Satan's "special forces" are able to spread out over the earth and wreak havoc in the lives of unbelievers. The Bible describes their ability to cause disease (Matthew 9:32; Luke 13:11, 16) as well as to take possession of non-Christians and animals (Matthew 4:24; Mark 5:13).

Against Christians

Satan and his demons are limited in their influence against believers. That's true for a couple of reasons. The first is that Christians are protected by the Holy Spirit, who is given to each of us at the moment of our salvation. Also, Jesus prays to the Father to protect us from the enemy (John 17:15).

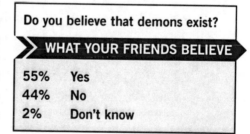

Do you believe that demons exist?

WHAT YOUR FRIENDS BELIEVE

55%	Yes
44%	No
2%	Don't know

However, that doesn't mean these supernatural spirits can't mess with us. They can't steal us from the Father (John 10:29), and they can't keep us out of heaven. But they can draw our attention away from the Father and tempt us to sin.

The father of lies loves to tempt Christians to lie, as well (Acts 5:3). He also tempts us to give in to sexual immorality (1 Corinthians 7:5) and uses our anger to get a foothold in our lives (Ephesians 4:27). When we give in, he goes running to God to make accusations and tell lies about us (Revelation 12:10). He also seeks to frustrate our attempts to do good things (1 Thessalonians 2:18), and works in the hearts of others to persecute us for following Jesus (Revelation 2:10).

In short, Satan is our enemy. He wants to destroy us. *Now.* Peter wrote that, "the devil prowls around like a roaring lion looking for someone to devour" (1 Peter 5:8). He knows he's in a battle he can't win, but that doesn't keep him from attacking.

Satan's Future

The devil's fate is sealed forever. It was locked in the moment Jesus walked out of his tomb alive. Here's what he has to look forward to:

- He will be completely banned from any access to God sometime during the Tribulation (Revelation 12:9).

- He will gather the governments of the world in the great battle of Armageddon against Jesus and his forces—and he will lose (Revelation 16:13-14).

- He'll be locked away in the abyss at the beginning of the millennium (Revelation 20:2).

- He'll be released for a short time, during which he'll use powerful deception to raise another army against God. Then he'll be utterly defeated and thrown into the lake of fire for all of eternity (Revelation 20:10).

Again, Satan and his demons know this is coming. One story in Matthew's Gospel describes a time Jesus was bravely walking near the tombs of the Gadarenes, an area everyone avoided because two violent demon-possessed men lived there. When they saw Jesus coming, the men yelled out, "What do you want with us, Son of God? Have you come here to torture us before the appointed time?" (Matthew 8:29)

These demons understood their time was coming, and that it wasn't yet. Knowing Jesus would cast them out of the men, they begged to be released into a herd of pigs. They needed something else to destroy. That's what Satan and his demons do—destroy. But they won't do it forever.

Now that we know a little more about Satan and the other fallen angels who work for him—and against believers— let's look at how we should (and shouldn't) interact with them.

CHAPTER 6: STANDING AGAINST THE DARKNESS

A few years ago, two highly skilled snipers caused panic in the region around Washington, D.C. by randomly killing people. Someone standing at a gas pump or putting bags in their car would be shot suddenly. No warning. They never saw it coming.

People I've talked to from the area said the fear and panic got so bad that some folks stayed home all the time. These snipers weren't taking out as many people as, say, someone using bombs. And they weren't doing it in as gruesome a way as some mass murderers. But they caused far more panic.

What freaked people out was the totally random nature of the killings. It could happen to anyone, anywhere, at any time. And there was nothing you could do to protect yourself. Well, almost nothing.

One newscast I saw featured interviews with some military-trained snipers. They said that a moving target is always harder for a sniper to hit than a target that is standing still. The best thing someone afraid of sniper fire could do, they said, was to run in a zigzag pattern any time they were in an exposed area.

The newscast then showed taped images of people going into a Wal-Mart doing exactly that. They were running from their cars to the building in a back-and-forth pattern until they got inside. I'll be honest. I thought they all looked kind of funny. But I wasn't in the sniper zone. I wasn't in danger of being hit.

Here's the question. If you truly believe in the supernatural—if you believe that Satan and his demons have declared war on you and that they're committed to tempting you, distracting you, leading you away from a life that makes a difference—what are you willing to do to protect yourself?

It comes back to worldview. People who have a worldview that says the supernatural world does not exist—that there is no God to answer to, no enemy to watch out for, no afterlife to worry about—won't care about how their choices impact their supernatural lives. They'll live in whatever way seems best for the visible world they can see around them.

People with a worldview that includes a loving supernatural God, an enemy hungry to "devour" them, and a future in the next life will live very differently. They will be aware that the hills are full of supernatural snipers, that they need to find ways to protect themselves, that their choices have consequences beyond what they can see.

Someone has said that Christians who ignore their supernatural enemy are "playing hopscotch in a war zone." If you don't want to be that foolish, how should you respond to and interact with Satan and demons?

67

Don't Live in Fear

It's true that Satan and his demons make war on humans, especially Christians. But it's also true that Christ has already won that war. Being serious about supernatural evil does not mean living in fear, afraid to do anything, because it might open us up to spiritual attack. As we'll see in the next few chapters, it does not mean blaming everything bad that happens in our lives on demonic activity.

Paul told Timothy that "God did not give us a spirit of timidity, but a spirit of power, of love and of self-discipline" (2 Timothy 1:7). Because God's own Holy Spirit lives with each Christian, we can stand against the enemy with confident power, love for one another, and self-discipline. In fact, the key to battling our fears of supernatural evil is to take that evil seriously.

How? First, remember that God's power is at work in you, and that he's already won. Next, join with other Christians regularly. Who is safer in a time of war, a lone soldier out on his own or a unit of troops working together? Living in loving relationships with other Christians, watching one another's backs, protects us from the fearful control of the enemy.

Paul's final reminder to Timothy was that timidity (or fear) is overcome by self-discipline. Soldiers who respect the enemy take time to discipline themselves through physical exercise, combat training, and studying the battle plan. We can also overcome fear by practicing the disciplines of the Christian life—regular prayer, Bible study, and memorization of Scripture.

Don't Flirt with Evil

Life often involves finding the balance between two extremes. C.S. Lewis once said, "Regarding the Devil we make one of two mistakes. We give him undue attention or we ignore him altogether."

On one hand, we don't need to fear the enemy and spend all our time obsessing about Satan and demonic activity. On the other hand, we can't afford to take Satan lightly, either. He is a "worthy adversary." Too many Christians make the mistake of treating the devil like a joke and thinking he has no real influence in their lives.

We get overconfident. We start thinking of movies about Satan and evil like *The Exorcist* and *The Ring* as exciting thrill rides instead of reflections of real darkness. We let our curiosity draw us into questionable books, music, or friendships, because we're intrigued by the dark power of the supernatural.

Acts 19:11-20 tells a true story about some men who took supernatural evil too lightly. They assumed they could control it, but discovered the truth in a scene straight out of a horror movie.

During the time of Christ and the early church age, supernatural activity was much more common. The existence of demons and their ability to possess people was widely accepted. Since magic and idol worship was also a big part of the culture, many so-called religious leaders and magicians offered spells and incantations to drive out spirits or to use spirits for human purposes.

One thing that got Paul and the other apostles so much attention was their real power over the supernatural through God. The power of most "magicians" was inconsistent. Sometimes, it seemed to work. Sometimes it didn't. Like today, many spiritists were just frauds trying to make money by fooling people with their fake power.

But Acts tells us the apostles were different:

> God did extraordinary miracles through Paul, so that even handkerchiefs and aprons that had touched him were taken to the sick, and their illnesses were cured and the evil spirits left them. (19:11-12)

Paul was a vehicle through which God's absolute power could work. The magicians of the day often relied on the power of demons—and demons are not required to obey men, as we'll see.

> Some Jews who went around driving out evil spirits tried to invoke the name of the Lord Jesus over those who were demon-possessed. They would say, "In the name of Jesus, whom Paul preaches, I command you to come out." Seven sons of Sceva, a Jewish chief priest, were doing this. (19:13-14)

Apparently, Paul's ability to cast out demons in the name of Jesus became so famous that other religious leaders started trying out Jesus' name and Paul's name to access that same power. But they weren't real believers in Jesus. It's possible that these sons of a Jewish chief priest were selling their demon-casting services for money.

One day the evil spirit answered them, "Jesus I know,

and I know about Paul, but who are you?" Then the man who had the evil spirit jumped on them and overpowered them all. He gave them such a beating that they ran out of the house naked and bleeding. (19:15-16)

Again, we see that demons recognize the name of Jesus. This one even knew Paul. What the demon said through this man he possessed was, "You have no power over me, because you don't come from Jesus." Then, with supernatural strength, the demon-possessed man attacked and brutally beat these seven men.

They took the real power of demons too lightly, and paid for their mistake in a terrible way. But look at how God used that evil event in the community:

When this became known to the Jews and Greeks living in Ephesus, they were all seized with fear, and the name of the Lord Jesus was held in high honor. Many of those who believed now came and openly confessed their evil deeds. A number who had practiced sorcery brought their scrolls together and burned them publicly. When they calculated the value of the scrolls, the total came to fifty thousand drachmas. In this way the word of the Lord spread widely and grew in power. (19:17-20)

The people who heard this story in a region full of supernatural activity had a very logical response—they were filled with fear. Yet they learned not only to respect the power of evil, but that Jesus was more powerful than demons. And many became followers of Christ.

They did something else, too. They stopped messing around with evil. People who were involved in demonic things gathered all their materials and burned them. They stopped flirting with darkness. They didn't want Satan or his demons to have any points of entry or influence in their lives.

How about you? If you had an experience like one of those seven men, would it be enough to convince you of the reality of Satan's power? Would you be motivated to get rid of (or stay away from) anything that *might* expose you to the enemy?

Satan and demons are just as real and powerful today as they were in Paul's day. They don't show themselves as often right now, partly because when people learn how real evil is, they tend to run into the safety of God's arms. But that doesn't mean those demons aren't active in the world.

Maybe it's time for you to quit flirting with evil and following your curiosity into books, music, Web sites, or other sources of information about evil. If you've already exposed yourself to that darkness, and if some of your possessions are connected with such evil, maybe you need to take more radical action and burn or destroy these items to get them out of your life.

Paul, known for his supernatural power through God, wrote this: "You were once in darkness, but now you are light in the Lord. Live as children of light...and find out what pleases the Lord. Have nothing to do with the fruitless deeds of darkness, but rather expose them" (Ephesians 5:8, 10-11).

Don't Mock, Insult, or Rebuke Satan

This one might surprise you, since Satan is our enemy. Some Christian teachers even instruct people to talk directly to Satan or demons and rebuke them in the name of Jesus. That's what

Jesus did, after all.

But the Bible seems to teach the exact opposite for followers of Jesus. Read what Jude wrote in the little book just before Revelation:

> In the very same way, these dreamers...slander celestial beings. But even the archangel Michael, when he was disputing with the devil...did not dare bring slanderous accusation against him, but said, "The Lord rebuke you!" Yet these men speak abusively against whatever they do not understand. (Jude 8-10)

I remember singing a little song in Sunday school: "If the devil doesn't like it, he can sit on a tack. Ouch!" Mocking or making fun of Satan in that way not only doesn't hurt him, it also makes him seem like a joke to us.

Our only power over Satan and demons is in God through Christ. So as the warrior angel Michael did, our best approach is to ask for God's help and protection over the devil—and let God take care of rebuking our enemy.

Be Watchful

Okay, so we're taking our enemy seriously and not mocking him. We're not living in fear, but we're also not dabbling in evil. The next step is to be watchful—aware of ways the enemy can trip us up even when we're trying to live right.

Remember, Satan's biggest weapon is deception. His favorite ploy is the sneak attack—getting you to turn from following God's path for you without letting you realize he's the one who's doing it.

Nearly every year, at least one person is killed in the mountains of Colorado by mountain lions. Several years ago, a young boy was hiking with his parents near Winter Park. He was playing a game by running up ahead of the group and hiding, then jumping out from behind a tree to scare them.

The last time he ran up ahead, the parents never expected to round the corner and find him laid out on the trail with his head in a mountain lion's mouth. It happened almost in an instant.

74   During certain times of year, mountain lions are more likely to attack people—especially the young or the injured. Does that mean nobody should ever go hiking up there? Nope. But the park service issues very strong warnings: Be watchful. Be ready. Don't assume there is no danger.

Remember that Peter compared Satan to a hungry lion looking for a meal: "Be self-controlled and alert. Your enemy the devil prowls around like a roaring lion looking for someone to devour" (1 Peter 5:8).

How does Satan "devour" us when we least expect it? Have you ever been moving ahead well in your relationship with God when a temptation pops up suddenly out of nowhere, and you give in to it almost without thinking? That's one way (1 Corinthians 7:5).

Another way he "jumps" us is to get our focus on how badly we've been treated. Ephesians 4:26-27 warns that holding on to bitterness and anger—looking for revenge—gives the devil a foothold in our lives.

The answer, again, is to remember that the enemy can work that way. Remain determined to make right choices in the power of the Holy Spirit. Don't let your guard down.

Resist Satan and Get Close to God

The very next verse Peter wrote after the "roaring lion" one says, "Resist him, standing firm in your faith" (1 Peter 5:9). And Jesus' half-brother, James, completed the thought: "Resist the devil, and he will flee from you" (James 4:7).

Bottom line: The devil can't stand toe to toe with God. As Christians, we have God's Spirit in us. We've been freed from Satan's grasp by Jesus' death for our sin. Satan can't control us.

So if you resist him—if you say no to temptation, if you reject rebellion against your parents, if you turn down alcohol and drugs, if you give up following your curiosity into darkness—he will run. That doesn't mean he's gone forever, but it does mean you can win every battle with him in the power of God's Spirit.

Part two comes in the next sentence in the same passage from James: "Come near to God and he will come near to you" (4:8). That's also a promise. The most powerful supernatural being in the world (much more powerful than Satan, whom God created) promises to get closer to us if we get close to him. And if God is close to us, Satan won't want to be around.

Suit Up and Take Your Stand

Probably the clearest instructions to Christians on how to deal with Satan and his demons come in Ephesians 6. There, Paul really drives home the reality of this invisible battle each and every Christian is in—whether we realize it or not:

> Put on the full armor of God so that you can take your stand against the devil's schemes. For our struggle is not against flesh and blood, but against the rulers, against the authorities, against the powers of this dark world and against the spiritual forces of evil in the heavenly realms. (Ephesians 6:11-12)

When Paul spells out what we're up against spiritually, it sounds dangerous. Satan and the fallen angels under him have power and authority on and around the earth. And since they're not a physical army, no amount of martial-arts training or stockpiled ammunition is going to help us.

We've got to get suited up for a spiritual battle; that means putting on God's spiritual armor and holding our spiritual ground:

> Stand firm then, with the belt of truth buckled around your waist, with the breastplate of righteousness in place, and with your feet fitted with the readiness that comes from the gospel of peace. In addition to all this, take up the shield of faith, with which you can extinguish all the flaming arrows of the evil one. Take the helmet of salvation and the sword of the Spirit, which is the word of God. And pray in the Spirit on all occasions with all kinds of prayers and requests. With this in mind, be alert and always keep on praying for all the saints. (6:14-18)

Belt of Truth

In Roman times, soldiers who wore robes or tunics would need to get them out of the way when it was time for battle. So they would gather the material together and tuck it into their belt. God's Word is the truth that holds us together spiritually. Study, memorization, and meditation in Scripture keep us from "tripping" over our lack of understanding of spiritual things.

Breastplate of Righteousness

When Isaiah saw the holiness of the angels in the throne room of God, he realized just how unrighteous he was. In fact, he thought he was going to die. He's the one who wrote that all our human righteous acts are like "filthy rags" (Isaiah 64:6). But when we're born again in Christ, God places his righteousness on us. Living in that righteousness protects us from Satan's attack.

Shoes of Readiness

Every soldier going into physical battle must struggle with whether or not he's ready to die. Because we're saved, we have peace in this life and in moving on to the next one. We have no reason to fear what our enemy can do to us.

Shield of Faith

There's a great illustration of this in the movie *Gladiator* starring Russell Crowe. A group of captured soldiers in the arena must fight for their lives against Roman soldiers with chariots. To do so, they form a circle, crouching down beneath their shields, which are nearly door-sized. When the arrows and spears of the enemies fly, the soldiers are protected.

The one soldier who leaves the protection of the shields and the group is quickly and easily run down and killed.

For Christians, God is our ultimate protection against our supernatural enemy. Trusting in him is our shield against the enemy's arrows of temptation, discouragement, bitterness, and confusion. Trusting ourselves more than God makes us vulnerable to the enemy's attacks.

Helmet of Salvation

Satan cannot destroy those who belong to God. As much as he'd like to devour us and send us to hell, we are protected where it really counts. Satan can't deliver the "death blow."

Sword of the Spirit

What weapon did Jesus use when Satan tried to tempt him in the wilderness? He quoted Scripture to counter Satan's lies with the truth.

Satan also wants to gain control of our lives through our minds, bodies, and emotions. God's Word is our one offensive weapon against the enemy. Knowing, understanding, and living by the Word limits Satan's ability to influence us.

Prayer

Paul doesn't picture prayer as a piece of armor. Instead, prayer is communication with our commanding officer and another source of protection. Simply continuing our ongoing conversation with God is a powerful defense against the enemy. Stopping that conversation for lengthy periods of time weakens us spiritually.

Pray for yourself and other Christians. Give thanks for everything. There is nothing too small or too unimportant to talk to the Father about.

Don't Be Duped

Now that we know more about what the Bible says about the supernatural world, we're ready to use our God-given discernment to separate the truth from the lies about the supernatural in our world.

79

We've gotten to know some of the players—God, angels, Satan, demons. But what can our knowledge of the Bible—and clear thinking—tells us about ghosts, vampires, and other supposedly spiritual entities? And how can we tell real supernatural events from hoaxes and coincidence?

In the next section of this book, we'll uncover six thinking traps that can lead Christians to wrong conclusions about the supernatural.

CHAPTER 7: EMOTIONS, PSYCHICS, AND GHOSTS

What we've uncovered in the last few chapters about God, angels, Satan, and demons are the basics of what Christians believe to be true about supernatural beings. Does that mean that nothing else exists in the supernatural world? Is there anything "out there" that the Bible doesn't describe?

We can't know for sure. But we *can* know that we can dismiss as untrue any ideas about the supernatural that contradict what the Bible teaches. Why? Because as Christians, we've made a choice to believe the teachings of the Bible. It's a reasonable faith. There's good evidence for the reliability of God's Word. But in the end, it's a choice to base our beliefs on a standard outside ourselves.

For people who believe the Bible, what Scripture teaches about the supernatural world is our standard.

So what do we do with all the other spiritual ideas in our culture today? What about Wiccans and witchcraft? How should we think about Native American spiritism and reincarnation and ghosts and communicating with the dead?

We've got to do two things with these and any other ideas about the supernatural that come our way. We've got to pass them through our discernment filter from chapter two—listen, learn, compare with Scripture (especially now that we know a little more about what Scripture teaches).

But we also have to remember that Satan's number one weapon in a Christian's life is deception. His plan, working through our culture and through his demons, is to confuse and mislead believers and unbelievers alike about the reality of the supernatural world.

Just because someone is religious and knows the Bible doesn't mean they can't be deceived. Remember what Jesus said to the some of the best-trained religious leaders of his day: "You belong to your father, the devil, and you want to carry out your father's desire. He was a murderer from the beginning, not holding to the truth, for there is no truth in him. When he lies, he speaks his native language, for he is a liar and the father of lies." (John 8:44)

Jesus actually told these men of high religious standing that they were Satan's kids! Why? Because they had believed the devil's lies. As the first and best liar, Satan's an expert and tripping up our thinking with both small and giant deceits.

Every supernatural experience or idea we come across has one of four possible explanations:

1. Spiritual activity from God. This would include events involving actual angels or godly intervention into the natural world.

2. Supernatural activity from Satan/demons. Events in this category would include actual demonic possession, demonic revelation, or other satanic/demonic influence on the natural world.

3. Hoax. Very often, experiences that appear to be supernatural—especially those involving someone on stage or otherwise making money from such event—are just cheap illusions. As an illusionist myself, I know how easy these are to pull off in highly believable ways.

4. Unexplained natural phenomena. We may mistake a natural experience for something supernatural. For instance, a person could believe that lights in the sky are from a UFO when, in fact, they are generated by an airplane or other human-created aircraft.

In the next few chapters, we'll dig into some of the most obvious thinking traps that can lead us to the wrong conclusions about the supernatural.

What supernatural events have you personally experienced?

> **WHAT YOUR FRIENDS BELIEVE**

16%	Presence/power of God
13%	Psychic or other supernatural events
12%	Averted or minimized damage from accidents
12%	Ghosts, angels, or other spiritual beings
8%	Supernatural healings
6%	Encounters with dead people
6%	Foretelling of the future
3%	Supernatural dreams

It's important to remember, though, that even when we discover that something is a hoax or just simple wrong thinking, it can still be used by Satan.

Satan's goal is to deceive you about the supernatural world. He loves to get skeptics to reject the reality of God (and himself) just as much as he loves to get those too eager to believe in the supernatural wrongly fascinated with lies about reincarnation, talking to the dead, and helpful spirit guides. Our goal is to find the truth in God, not just to reject everything in the supernatural world.

Thinking Trap #1: Not Balancing Mind with Emotions

The death of a loved one may be the most emotional experience in life. Even Christians who carry the hope of meeting that person again in heaven often carry the intense pain of loss for many years. The pain and longing can be amplified when some key issue in the relationship remains unresolved. Supposed spiritists and psychics have been exploiting those emotions to take advantage of people for thousands of years.

"I feel someone coming through. He's very assertive. He really wants you to know something. Is there a...an "R" in your family?"

A woman gasps. "Richard? Richard was my uncle! My father's brother."

"Yes. Yes, I'm getting that. R is very strong. He wants you to know something about your dad. I'm getting something about the chest area or...Is there something about the chest?"

"My dad died of heart disease."

"Yes, that's it. That's it. And there's more. Something about a...a car or a truck..."

"I don't know. Hmmm. Well, my dad did give me a car for my sixteenth birthday."

"Right. I'm getting that Richard wants you to know that your dad is okay about the car. Was there a problem with the car?"

84 "Well, I didn't really like it. Dad might have felt bad when I sold it."

"I'm getting strongly from Richard that your dad wants you to know that everything's okay. He's okay."

The woman is crying now. "And there's something about a nephew or a niece? Someone below you. A child?"

"My son Daniel would be Robert's nephew."

"Right. Of course. R is emphatic that the child will be okay. You don't have to worry about him."

The woman is crying harder now, and she's convinced that a spiritually gifted psychic has just given her a message from her father and uncle beyond the grave. It's very moving for her—and even for those who are watching her remember and think about her passed loved ones.

If you read that exchange carefully, though, you'll see

that the psychic didn't really know anything about the woman's life that she didn't tell him. I personally know highly skilled illusionists that can convince entire audiences of their psychic abilities using similar fishing and reflecting techniques. It's not that hard.

In addition, it's now very easy to get basic information about people from the Internet. Shows like *Crossing Over with John Edwards* and *Pet Psychic* could easily utilize information provided when someone buys a ticket to the show to find out all kinds of things about an audience member's past. A little conversation while waiting in line to see the show with a friendly stranger (who works for the psychic) could also reveal a lot.

85

Combine that kind of basic digging with some of the "cold reading" skills of psychic illusion—the power of suggestion, selective memory, fishing for and repeating information as if you came up with it—and you can create a spookily convincing psychic presentation.

Why do many people buy it? Why are people in the audience and at home tricked into believing the psychic is really delivering messages from the afterlife?

Emotion. When it comes to the areas where our feelings are deepest, humans are very vulnerable creatures. If I show up to a psychic hoping to hear from my dead mother, I'm already emotional. If you can give me just enough convincing-sounding comments from her that I assume you could never have known, I'm likely to believe she's speaking through you. And I'm likely to pay you for more information.

What is it about our emotions that can prevent our minds

from working well? The Bible says, "The heart is deceitful above all things and beyond cure. Who can understand it?" (Jeremiah 17:9). But that doesn't mean our emotions are evil. They're just very powerful; we need to learn to control our emotions instead of letting them run away with us.

"Above all else," says Proverbs, "guard your heart, for it is the wellspring of life" (4:23).

Guarding our hearts means being aware that our emotions may lead us away from truth and from God's best direction for us. That's why the first step in guarding our hearts is to fill them with God's truth—learning to trust God instead of the way that "feels" best to us.

Psalm 37 reminds us that when the law of God is in our hearts, our feet will not slip (37:31). And Proverbs urges, "Trust in the LORD with all your heart and lean not on your own understanding; in all your ways acknowledge him, and he will make your paths straight" (Proverbs 3:5-6).

So avoiding the thinking trap of letting our emotions rule our minds comes down to trusting God's Word, even when our emotions tell us to believe something else.

Ghosts, Spirits, and Reincarnation

And what, exactly, does the Bible teach about life after death—and spirits reaching out from beyond the grave? It doesn't leave much room for such things to happen.

The writer of Hebrews said, "Just as man is destined to die once, and after that to face judgment..." (Hebrews 9:27).

That at least implies that death is followed by facing God, not by hanging around on earth in spirit form. It definitely rules out reincarnation for those who believe the Bible (since people die only once). And Paul wrote about his willingness to be absent from the body and present with the Lord (2 Corinthians 5:8), suggesting that for Christians, one immediately follows the other.

So even though I might feel strong emotions about getting a message from "the spirits all around us," including one from a lost loved one, I have to compare that idea to what the Bible teaches. And Scripture doesn't seem to teach that the spirits of lost loved ones can contact me through psychics.

Beyond that, we do believe the Bible leaves room for the possibility that Satan or demons could use a psychic to fool people into believing they were talking to the dead. Many psychics claim to be hearing voices or becoming possessed by the spirits of those they are "channeling." Though these claims are most often a hoax, it's at least possible that demons are involved in these processes.

That might be why God commanded the Israelites to avoid getting involved with such people: "Do not turn to mediums or seek out spiritists, for you will be defiled by them" (Leviticus 19:31). Such contact could open a person up to demonic influence.

Only one passage in the Bible suggests contact with the dead is even possible—and even this story seems to suggest that things like that don't happen normally. It's the story of King Saul and the witch of Endor (1 Samuel 28).

Saul was on the decline as king, and he knew it. He was afraid the Philistines were about to crush his army. So he called on God for some reassurance. But God wouldn't answer Saul.

So even though Saul had earlier had all the mediums and spiritists removed from the country, Saul's men somehow found one in Endor, and Saul went to see her in disguise. He wanted to talk to the prophet Samuel, who had died. But he had to swear to the witch in God's name that she wouldn't be punished if she did it. The king was willing to break his own law in order to find emotional reassurance from someone who had died.

When the witch did her thing, she cried out in surprise when she somehow suddenly became aware that Saul was the king. She said that she saw an old man rising out of the ground in a robe, and she delivered a disturbing message from Samuel to Saul that started out with the words, "Why have you disturbed me by bringing me up?" (1 Samuel 28:15).

The message that followed from Samuel is apparently something only Samuel and Saul (and God) would have known about. And it left Saul in greater terror than before he had come to the witch.

It's unclear exactly what happened in the witch's house that night, but Bible scholars suggest several possibilities:

Some suggest the woman was just pulling a hoax on Saul in order to give him what he wanted. However, it seems unlikely she would have known what Samuel told Saul.

Others say the woman was possessed by a demon who delivered the message to Saul through the woman. That's possible, since she was a witch in a time when there was much spirit worship. But the passage doesn't say anything about Samuel not really being Samuel.

A third idea—and the one that seems most likely—is that this witch intended to do a hoax, but got more than she expected. Perhaps she normally tricked people the way most psychics and mediums do today. The fact that she cries out in a loud voice when Samuel appears suggests that she was shocked and surprised to actually hear from someone who had "crossed over."

It's definitely possible that God used this means as a one-time supernatural event to communicate his message to Saul through a deceased prophet who had been used many times to deliver supernatural messages. But this example does not suggest that it's "normally" possible to talk with the spirits of humans who have passed on. In fact, it seems to suggest that only through God's power could such a thing happen.

Emotions are wonderful and powerful, but we can't trust feelings to run our lives. And we really can't trust them to help us make right decisions about the world of the supernatural. Instead, God calls us to give our emotions to him and trust what his Word teaches us about the spiritual universe.

In the next chapter, we'll look at three more thinking traps that lead people to wrong conclusions about the supernatural.

CHAPTER 8: FEARS, HALF-TRUTHS, AND PARTIAL PERSPECTIVES

Not every deception—or thinking trap—that we fall into comes from our enemy, the devil. As an illusionist, I've trained with some of the best human deceivers in the world. They have taught me how to use human nature against itself in order to perform the most effective illusions. The fact is: We humans aren't that hard to fool. Unless we learn to think clearly and carefully, we're easily trapped into thinking the wrong things.

It's one thing to be fooled by a skilled illusionist who makes it seem like a playing card magically appeared in your back pocket or that he somehow read your mind. It's much more dangerous to allow ourselves to be fooled in our thinking about the supernatural world.

What we need is something we haven't talked a lot about yet in this book—wisdom. Wisdom is the ability to understand what's going on in our lives and in the world around us. Wisdom is not about being smart, necessarily. It's not about getting perfect scores on your S.A.T.

Wisdom is the ability to use what you know to figure out

the best things to believe and do. When it comes to understanding the supernatural world, we need a lot of wisdom. The Bible tells us that King Solomon, David's son, was the wisest man who ever lived. The Book of Proverbs is full of his wise sayings. And from him, we get some important clues about finding wisdom.

First, wisdom starts with respecting the fact that God is God (Proverbs 1:7). As we discovered in chapter three, unless you accept that God exists and that he's in control, you start with the wrong worldview. Believing that there is no God is foolish and leaves us open to all kinds of deception (Psalm 53:1).

Next, wisdom is worth sacrificing for. Better to risk everything we have to get wisdom—and live wisely—than to take the easy road and believe a lie about spiritual things (Proverbs 3:11-20).

Finally, anyone willing to look for wisdom can find it in three different ways. One, wisdom comes from experience—especially from getting burned by believing a lie. Someone who has lost money on a scam is much less likely to believe the same scam the next time. Wise people learn from the consequences of their actions (Proverbs 21:11).

Two, wisdom comes from studying God's Word. We've already seen that the Bible is part of the armor of God—a weapon against the deceits of our supernatural enemy. It's also the key to being wise enough to reject easy lies about spiritual things. God's Word turns simple people into wise people (Psalm 19:7). Building it into our lives is critical to not being duped by supernatural deceit.

Three, God hands out wisdom for free to everyone who

asks him for it. You might think that's the easiest way to avoid being a fool—but Jesus' half-brother James wrote that you have to ask God for wisdom *knowing* he's able to give it to you (James 1:5-8). Still, what an amazing thing that God is willing to give us the wisdom to avoid dangerous thinking traps—for free.

Why do we need wisdom? Because we're so easy to fool. Let's look at some more of the thinking traps that trip us up in the area of beliefs about the supernatural.

Thinking Trap #2: Partial Perspective

92 Magicians and illusionists use this technique to fool people all the time. If we showed you everything that was going on—what was happening behind our backs or up our sleeves or within the hand you're not looking at—the trick wouldn't work at all. The deception works because you see only part of what's going on.

It's like the old poem called "The Blind Men and the Elephant" by John Godfrey Saxe. Based on a fable told in India, it describes six blind men going to "see" an elephant for the first time. Led around the elephant, each grabbed a different part of it to see what the elephant was like.

Of course, each person had a different "experience" of the elephant. One felt the broad side and thought it was like a wall. Another felt the tusk and thought elephants must be like spears. Another felt the elephant's trunk; the others a leg, an ear, and the tail—and each decided, in turn, that elephants must be like snakes, trees, large fans, or ropes.

Because each man decided what elephants are like based on his own experience alone, none of them got it right. They were all deceived.

Solomon expressed a similar idea in Proverbs 18:17: "The first to present his case seems right, till another comes forward and questions him." It happens with rumors all the time. You hear a little piece of a story that gives you one idea—usually a nasty

Which of these psychic activities have you taken part in?

> **WHAT YOUR FRIENDS BELIEVE**

79%	Read your horoscope
35%	Used a Ouija board
34%	Read a book about witchcraft or Wicca
30%	Had your palm read
28%	Played a game that involved witchcraft/psychic elements
27%	Had your fortune told
14%	Been present when someone used psychic/supernatural power
10%	Participated in a séance
9%	Visited a medium or spirit guide
9%	Called or saw a psychic
8%	Tried to cast a spell or mix a magical potion

one. Later, you hear the whole story and realize that your partial perspective completely distorted the truth.

On the few occasions when I've revealed the secret to one of my illusions, some people have become very angry with me. They can't believe the illusion that baffled them so much actually has such an easy and simple solution. They end up feeling foolish for being tricked by something that's really simple and straightforward. When they know the whole truth, their original confusion seems silly.

But it's not silly. It's just that these people only had a partial perspective.

The same often happens with our ideas about supernatural things, both with hoaxes and with actual spiritual events. Because we see only part of what's going on, we leap to the wrong conclusions.

Psychics on TV use this technique, too. Often, such shows simply edit out all the stuff they get wrong and splice together the clips of the stuff that "worked." When you don't see the misses, the hits strung together can look pretty impressive.

You can fall into a similar trap when you try to figure out the truth about actual supernatural events based only on your experience. You have a partial perspective. Whether you say, "I've never experienced anything supernatural," or "I once experienced something really weird," you saw only part of the elephant. You can't make any conclusions from your one small corner of the universe.

In the end, you have to rely on God's Word to give you

the whole story—and his wisdom to give you the ability to sort out your experiences.

Thinking Trap #3: Fear and Insecurity

Sometimes, our ability to think wisely is clouded by intense fear of the supernatural or deep insecurities about ourselves. It happens to all of us.

When I was initially working on this material, I was teaching at a conference in California. The people hosting the conference let me stay at a beautiful cabin they had deep in the woods. Unfortunately, I was there by myself, and I didn't have a car. And I didn't get there until way after dark.

Alone in the woods. In the dark. Thinking about angels and demons and ghosts. I got a little creeped out, but I tried to keep my emotions calm. I was doing okay until I went to bed and started listening. I kept hearing strange sounds coming from inside the closet, and then I felt a cool breeze flowing out from under the closet door.

You may have guessed by now that I have a pretty active imagination. With all the stuff I'd been studying, I started thinking maybe this was some kind of supernatural experience. Maybe I was under attack from the enemy. Now I was really freaking out. I felt paralyzed by my fear.

Finally, after what seemed like hours, I found the courage to get up and look in that closet. I *had* to know what was really going on. When I opened the door, I discovered that this newly finished cabin in the woods had a trap door in the floor that had been left open. I could see straight down to the ground under the cabin. The sounds and cold I was feeling were coming from outside. After I closed the trap door, I felt a little silly—and quite relieved!

Because of my fear (and extreme fatigue), my imagination had jumped to conclusions about the supernatural. Sometimes, Christians are even more likely to do this than non-Christians. Because we allow for the possibility of supernatural good and evil, we become afraid of such forces even when there's no evidence that the supernatural is involved at all.

I've experienced the other side of this as well. When I was in college at Biola University, I tried out a mind-reading trick on a few other students. The trick worked really well, and none of them could figure out how I was able to "read their minds." Of course, I didn't read anyone's mind. It was a trick.

However, one girl got really freaked out. She couldn't stop thinking about what she had experienced, and finally someone told me she thought I had supernatural demonic powers. I decided to go to her and show her exactly how I had done the trick so she wouldn't be afraid any more. We eventually became good friends, but her fear made her suspicious of me for many months.

At the PlanetWisdom conferences, I repeat over and over that every illusion I perform is a trick. I don't have any supernatural powers. Still, some Christians are so fearful of supernatural things that they become afraid of me because I do tricks they can't figure out. Their fear blinds them to the truth about the supernatural.

So how do we keep from falling into the trap of being deceived by our fear of the supernatural? For one, don't feed the fear. Many TV shows, books, and movies build their audiences by scaring them. Horror movies. Slasher films. Violent detective fiction. Even TV shows like *Law & Order* and *C.S.I.* bring people back for repeated viewings by thrilling them with frightening images and ideas.

If such movies and shows stir up fear in you, don't keep feeding it by watching them. The thing you fear most might not actually be from Satan or demons, but those beings can use your fear to steal the joyful confidence of walking with God.

Satan can also use our insecurity about ourselves to deceive us into believing crazy things about the supernatural. A few years ago, a group of highly intelligent and wealthy people killed themselves in a really bizarre way. They were all found dead in a luxury house near San Diego, with buzz cuts and white tennis shoes, their faces and chests covered with a purple cloth.

It turned out that the group believed they were going to be taken up to the "kingdom of heaven" in conjunction with the approach of the Hale-Bopp comet if they died in a specific way at a specific time. Why would these smart people believe such things?

Partly, they were drawn into the Heaven's Gate cult because many of them were insecure about themselves. Among the other members of the cult, they found acceptance, what felt like love, and the illusion of meaning. To hold on to that, they were willing to believe very strange things about the supernatural. Satan was able to use their fears and insecurities to blind their minds to the truth.

As Christians, we don't need to live in fear. Psalm 49:5 says, "Why should I fear when evil days come, when wicked deceivers surround me?" In fact, we can walk in confidence that we belong to God and he meets all of our needs.

Believers can understand the truth about good and evil in the supernatural world without living in fear of it or always assuming that everything they don't understand is evil. Even in dark and evil times, we can know that God is in control. "Even though I walk through the valley of the shadow of death, I will fear no evil, for you are with me; your rod and your staff, they comfort me" (Psalm 23:4).

How do we conquer fear? By trusting in God's power to save us. He will give us the courage to defeat our fears and the wisdom to discover the truth: "I sought the LORD, and he answered me; he delivered me from all my fears" (Psalm 34:4).

Thinking Trap #4: Truth Mixed with Lies

Every person who has ever successfully lied to his or her parents on a regular basis knows how powerful this thinking trap can be.

"Yes, I was at Kate's house all night. We were studying. No, there weren't any boys there. It just took us longer than we thought to get the project done."

Well, you were at Kate's house, but not *all* night. And you did study just long enough to be able to say "we studied" without completely lying. And the boys that were there didn't actually come into the house; so that wasn't a total lie.

It's the truth in the middle of the story that makes the lies so easy to swallow, isn't it? This technique is one of Satan's best moves. And he's much better at it than any of us ever will be.

Remember how the serpent lied to Eve in the garden? "Did God really say, 'You must not eat from any tree in the garden'?" (Genesis 3:1)

He didn't start with a lie, really—just a question that assumed something untrue was true. He knew it wasn't the case, of course. But he wanted to get Eve's mind going. She corrected him with the truth that only one tree was off-limits, that eating from it would kill them.

He responded with a lie wrapped up in just enough truth to make it believable: "You will not surely die. For God knows that when you eat of it your eyes will be opened, and you will be like God, knowing good and evil" (3:4-5).

And he was partly right, wasn't he? Adam and Eve didn't die immediately, and they did get a sudden rush of knowing evil. But they did die eventually. And they did die spiritually. Satan's mix of lie and truth was just right to get the results he was aiming for.

David Koresh, leader of the Branch Davidian cult in Waco, Texas, used a similar approach to convince people of his lies. (Or maybe he was just used by Satan in a similar way.) His cult started as a Bible study. Like evangelical Christians everywhere, he taught that the Bible was God's standard for truth.

Then slowly, over time, he began to mix in some lies with the truth. His followers eventually accepted whoppers like, "All the virgins need to have sex with me," because they were brought along with just enough truth along the way to convince them this cult leader was a man of God. And the end was the same: destruction.

In the world of the supernatural, many people follow a piece of truth into mighty big lies. Understanding that angels are real spiritual beings created by God to serve his children (which we've learned to be true from God's Word), they start to wonder what else angels do. When someone tells them that angels are available to serve us if we pray to them, they think they'd like to experience that.

And when good things happen after praying to angels, they begin to believe the angels are responsive to their prayers. Soon, it's not hard to make the jump to building altars to angels and using spells to call them to yourself. Some people even claim to have experienced hearing "angel's voices" telling them what to do.

The scary thing about these lies mixed with truth is that "Satan himself masquerades as an angel of light" (2 Corinthians 11:14). Once we wander from the truth and start exploring unbiblical ideas about the supernatural, we're ripe targets for deception and destruction.

The key to avoiding this thinking trap, of course, is to know the truth so well that the lies stick out like sore thumbs. Studying, memorizing, and meditating on God's Word results in being aware of the contradictions to it when we hear them. The more we know the truth, the more jarring the lies will become.

That's what God's wisdom is all about.

In the next chapter, we'll explore three more thinking traps that lead us away from the truth about spiritual things.

CHAPTER 9: WISHES, FACTS, AND FALSE ASSOCIATIONS

In this chapter, we'll seek to shine the bright light of wisdom and clear thinking on three more thinking traps. As we do so, it's important to remember why we're doing this. In a time when more and more people are willing to believe more and more things about the supernatural world, we don't want to be deceived.

Like all good traps, these thinking traps don't look like trouble when you come up on them. The rope that will grab you by the ankles and hoist you into the air is hidden under the leaves on the path. The hole in the ground that's full of sharp sticks waiting to skewer you is covered with enough sticks to look like solid ground.

The thing about a good trap is that you don't know it's there until it gets you—unless you know what to look for. Here are three more things to look for as you try to sort out truth from lies regarding the supernatural world around you.

Thinking Trap #5: Wishful Thinking

This trap always looks good, because we create it with our own minds. What do you most *want* to be true? That's what this trap looks like.

The people I know who work as "psychic entertainers" are very aware of exactly what most people in their audience want. They want to hear that their dead friends and relatives are okay. They want to find true love or to hear that they are loved by the people whom they love. They want to hear that they're going to have success in their careers or make a lot of money. They want to know that they're going to be healthy or healed of illness.

So there's no end to the phony psychics on 800 numbers and TV shows and tarot card booths who use the skills we've talked about in previous chapters to "supernaturally reveal" exactly what their paying customers want to hear. They start by just quietly listening while their victims reveal more about themselves than they realize, then they "connect with the spirits" to tell those folks exactly what they hope to hear.

Someone who desperately wants something to be true is willing to overlook even the most obvious errors to get the confirmation and comfort they're looking for.

Unfortunately, it's not just fake psychics and mind readers who are guilty of using this technique to deceive. Religious teachers have been caught doing the same thing. They know that Christians long for "proof" of the reality of God, and that many are desperate to experience supernatural things.

Some of these deceivers intentionally mislead Christians and religious people in order to make money. Others seem to believe that they're receiving supernatural power from God when they're not. But men and women with both good and bad motivations have been used of Satan to deceive too many people about God's power.

Telling a lie that seems to support God is no better than telling a lie that seems to be against him. Faking a supernatural healing and claiming that it's from God is still a lie. And all lies are against God.

Remember one more time what Jesus said to the religious leaders of his day. He called them the children of Satan because they were lying to their followers about God. I'm sure many of them thought they were telling the truth. Others may have known they were lying to protect their power and their money (just like some of today's false TV preachers). But all were equally guilty of speaking Satan's language.

Christians today need to use just as much wisdom and discernment in judging whether religious leaders are telling the truth about the supernatural as in accessing the supernatural ideas that come from TV, movies, and other entertainment sources.

Why? Because we can be just as guilty about wishful thinking in the area of supernatural things as unbelievers are. We want to believe that sick person was healed in that service to show God's power. We want to believe an angel stepped in at the last minute to keep that person alive. And those things *can* happen. I believe they *do* happen sometimes. But that doesn't mean they happen every time we're told they do by religious leaders.

It's okay to ask hard questions about such supernatural claims. One famous Bible teacher on the radio has made a practice of asking for before-and-after medical records for people who claim to have been supernaturally healed. That's okay. If God is revealing his very real supernatural power in that way to the world, it should be verifiable. We should exhaust the other explanations about supernatural experiences before jumping to the conclusion that it could only have been supernaturally of God.

Does that mean we don't have enough faith? No, exactly the opposite. Because we are so confident God can do supernaturally powerful things, we don't want his reputation tarnished by claims that fakes and accidents are actually his work. We don't have to wish and hope God is real. We know he is, whether we "experience" a supernatural event or not.

Why is this such a big deal? Because way too many people have been turned away from Christ by "Christian" liars who claimed obviously natural things were supernatural—many of whom were getting rich in the process. With real Christians, the truth should always come first—especially about supernatural things.

Thinking Trap #6: Bad Source

Another trap that both Christians and unbelievers fall into is that of believing something they've read or heard without first checking out the source. If something really happened, we should always be able to trace it back to the source.

For example, when I got one of those mass e-mails telling me that my friend Bart from the Christian worship band Mercy

Me had been killed, I went straight to the source. I called him on his cell phone and asked him. He denied it.

Here's a more serious example that also involves e-mail. When the *Harry Potter* books were first growing in popularity—and many news stories were reporting that millions of children were reading them—an e-mail was circulated through the Christian community faster than a prayer chain about the pastor. The e-mail was a copy of a "news" story about Potter author J. K. Rowling. It quoted her as saying that she was, in fact, a witch, and that she wrote the Potter books to recruit youngsters into exploring the real and exciting world of witchcraft. It also told about groups of little kids who were dabbling with pentagrams and casting spells.

How many people got that e-mail? How many repeated that story to others, outraged that Christians were letting their kids read those books? How many actually took the time to chase down the source of the story? Those who did found out it was written by a satire newspaper and Web site called *The Onion*. It was completely bogus. The whole thing was meant to be a joke. It turned out that the joke was on Christians who believed and spread the lie.

For the record, J. K. Rowling is not a witch. Her stated intent with the books is not to recruit new witches and warlocks. Does that mean we shouldn't wrestle with the issue of consuming books and movies about witchcraft? No. Christians need to decide if and how they'll take in such content. But telling each other lies about those things because we don't take the time to check out the source leads us straight into a thinking trap.

Here's another example: One day, a guy I was discipling came running into my office very excited. He said his friend had just had an amazing experience with an angel of God. This friend had picked up a hitchhiker along the highway. The hitchhiker told the friend that he was, in fact, an angel sent to earth to warn people that Jesus was coming back in a week. Then the hitchhiker vanished right before his eyes.

My friend told me that the guy pulled off the highway and went straight to a 7-Eleven to call his wife on a pay phone. While he was telling his wife the story, the guy behind the counter got the weirdest look on his face. When he hung up, the clerk told him he was the fifth person to tell the exact same story on that pay phone.

My friend was so excited. Jesus was coming back next week. We had to spread the word. I told him I wanted to show him something. In my office is a book of urban legends. I showed him the story he had just told me; it's been around for more than 20 years. My friend's face fell. Then I suggested we check the source by calling his friend right away.

When we did, his friend said, "Well, it didn't actually happen to me; it happened to my friend." So we called my friend's friend's friend. "Well, it wasn't really me; it was this guy I know." Turns out that it didn't happen to anyone we could find in the real world. It was like that old song, "Heard it from a friend who heard it from a friend who…"

Wisdom demands that when it comes to figuring out the truth about the supernatural world, we chase down the sources of our information with the ferocity of a good journalist. If we can't find a source—or if the source is questionable—we shouldn't just assume the story is true.

Thinking Trap #7: False Associations

This one could be categorized under the heading of "superstition," but most of us have been guilty of it at one time or another.

Athletes do it. If the team wins a couple games in a row while one player is wearing the same pair of socks, he may decide those socks are "lucky" and choose to wear them for every big game. That's a false association. Those socks have nothing to do with who wins or loses (unless their stench overpowers the other team).

Sometimes even scientists do it. Every scientist learns early on that "correlation doesn't equal causation," but even they may find it hard not to leap to conclusions. If a study indicates that people who drink more water also have fewer headaches, can we assume that drinking water reduces headaches? It sounds good. But it's not necessarily true. Just because two things happen together doesn't mean one causes the other.

Try this one. The amount that humans perspire is greater in months when mosquitoes are the most active. Therefore, we can conclude that mosquitoes cause people to sweat, right? Of course not. It's true that in summer, there are both more mosquitoes and more people sweating. But neither one causes the other. It's a false association. Correlation (two things happening together) does not equal causation (one causing the other).

I fell headfirst into this thinking trap when I was a kid.

My great-grandmother was in the hospital with a serious illness. Mom asked if I wanted to go with the family to visit her. I said no, thinking I'd have another chance. She died.

Later, the same thing happened with my grandfather. Did I want to go see him or stay home with my brothers? I stayed home, and he died. In my warped, little-kid brain, I made an association. When I don't visit people in the hospital, they die.

The next time I had a grandpa in the hospital for a big surgery, I didn't miss one chance to visit him. And—ta da!—he lived. I decided that I had the supernatural power over life and death. When I visited people in the hospital they lived. When I did not, they died. My mission in life would be to visit people in the hospital and save their lives.

Eventually, I had to admit that I'd made a false association. Why? Because people I went to see did die. Others I never got a chance to visit lived without my help. Apparently, my presence or absence had no effect on human mortality, after all.

In the area of the supernatural, we might assume that the words "abra cadabra" are magic, because something amazing happens every time a magician says that phrase. Or we could assume that because our horoscope said, "You will encounter an interesting individual," the same month that we met a new boyfriend, the horoscope was predicting our future. That's a false association.

Our survey of the supernatural beliefs of U.S. teenagers revealed that 79 percent had consulted a horoscope at least once, and 53 percent thought that they might be true. A whopping 24 percent said that horoscopes are probably mostly true. That's a lot of teenagers buying into the reality of these false prophets.

Horoscope writers are highly skilled at writing things that could be true, in part, for large numbers of people. They rely heavily on the thinking trap of false associations (and wishful thinking) to trick people into believing they have the power to tell the future.

And Satan uses that belief in a lie to lead people away from relying on the God who controls the future. That's why the Bible is so specific in telling us to avoid fortune tellers and mediums.

In the next chapter, we're going to meet a spiritual being we haven't talked that much about. You might be surprised to find out who it is.

CHAPTER 10: THE MOST COMMON SUPERNATURAL BEING

There's one supernatural, spiritual entity that we haven't spent much time talking about in this book. It's probably the most common spiritual being ever created. We've all met one. In fact, we've met hundreds. We call them humans.

According to our standard, God's Word, we humans are more than just skin and bones and fat tissue driven by the electrochemical firings of the grey stuff in our skulls. There's more to us than just the physical. We are also spiritual beings.

The Bible teaches that each of us is created in the image of God (Genesis 1:27). We can think and imagine and create and make choices. We are born with souls, and this deepest part of us allows us to connect to God and communicate with him.

But since the Garden of Eden, there has been a problem. Sin separates us from God. And disconnected from our Source, our spirits wither away and die—unless something very powerful happens.

In George Romero's classic, much imitated and often

spoofed 1968 horror film, *Night of the Living Dead*, people rise up out of their graves and walk like, well, zombies as they slowly, haltingly stagger around in search of human flesh. By today's standards, the movie is kind of low-tech and goofy. But the image of those decaying zombies walking through the streets with their arms stretched out in front of them is one that's hard to shake.

I wonder if Romero ever read this passage from Ephesians about the spiritual nature of human beings without Christ:

> And you were dead in your trespasses and sins, in which you formerly walked according to the course of this world, according to the prince of the power of the air, of the spirit that is now working in the sons of disobedience. (Ephesians 2:1-2, NASB)

Dead people walking. That's what Paul said we were. The "prince of the power of the air" is Satan, who rules our planet to the extent that God lets him. The picture here, then, is that people without Christ are the walking dead, ruled by the fallen angel Satan and his demons.

What a spooky image! And we've all been there:

> All of us also lived among them at one time, gratifying the cravings of our sinful nature and following its desires and thoughts. Like the rest, we were by nature objects of wrath. (2:3)

Like those zombies, walking mindlessly in search of human flesh, people without Christ are controlled by their "cravings." Before Christ, we longed for sinful things. We were driven to satisfy our way, to get what we wanted in every area of life.

And like those zombies, we were doomed. By the end of the horror movie that is life on earth without God, we were sure to be tossed into the supernatural fires of hell—not to cease to exist, but for our empty souls to live forever in torment. (More on that in the next chapter.)

But then a hero came to save us. To wake us up. To bring us to spiritual life.

112

> But because of his great love for us, God, who is rich in mercy, made us alive with Christ even when we were dead in transgressions—it is by grace you have been saved. And God raised us up with Christ and seated us with him in the heavenly realms in Christ Jesus, in order that in the coming ages he might show the incomparable riches of his grace, expressed in his kindness to us in Christ Jesus. (2:4-7)

God didn't send this hero after the zombies all got together and decided they'd really rather be alive than dead. There's was no zombie petition drive to get God to rescue us from continually chasing our sinful desires right into the gates of hell. As zombies, we would never have asked for such a thing. We were dead.

So God sent the hero before we knew we needed one. And this hero was different. He was like us—a human with a soul and emotions and thoughts—but he wasn't born a zombie. He was spiritually alive, because he didn't inherit the zombie disease, sin. He never sinned, so he never died spiritually.

That's why he could pay the price for the sin that all of us zombies—the walking dead—had earned. He became the object of God's wrath in our place. That's why the only way to be freed from this zombie existence is to trust in Jesus:

> For it is by grace you have been saved, through faith—
> and this not from yourselves, it is the gift of God—not
> by works, so that no one can boast. (2:8-9)

We can't earn our way to being alive. As zombies, there's no way for us to try really hard to be less evil than the other zombies. "I ate half as much human flesh as all the other zombies; surely God will be impressed and make me alive!"

No matter what you've heard from other religions about the supernatural world, it doesn't work that way. Good works *can't* save us. We have to be made alive by God through trusting in Jesus. He has to do it for us, because we could never do it for ourselves. Zombies just don't spring to life by themselves.

But the moment a believer trusts in Jesus, everything changes. He or she suddenly becomes alive in Christ. We're not dead anymore. Our zombie days are behind us. Like Jesus when he was on earth, we're alive. Alive!

God calls it grace—a free gift. In spite of the fact that we had earned death and hell, he wants to give us life now and the unimaginable riches of being in heaven with Jesus forever. (More on that in the next chapter, too.)

Supernatural Power

Although we don't talk about it with this language very often, those made alive in Christ have way more going for them than just being heaven-bound. We're given incredible supernatural powers.

Amazingly, some Christians aren't really interested in these supernatural gifts of power and ability from God. They don't want really want to hear about all that. They'd rather think of themselves as Batman than Superman.

Batman is different from most of the other superheroes, because he doesn't have any supernatural powers. Maybe that's one reason he's so popular. Using his mind, his own strength, his incredible wealth, and tons of cool high-tech gear, he's able to defeat the bad guys. Lots of Christians want to lead their Christian lives that way.

114   Yes, God saved them, and they know they needed his supernatural power to get to heaven. But in the meantime—between now and heaven—they'll handle things on their own. After all, they're pretty smart, and they still have some things they want to try. They've decided that they'll just take it easy on the supernatural stuff until this life is over.

How sad! God has given Christians amazing supernatural abilities. We don't have to settle for using our limited wits and strength to take on the world. We can live like Clark Kent on the WB show *Smallville*.

In case you haven't seen *Smallville*, it tells the story of Superman's life as a teenager growing up on the plains of Kansas. Not only does he have supernatural strength and speed, every few episodes he discovers new powers he didn't know he had. For the longest time, he didn't even realize he could fly.

And what does he do with all these powers? Good! He does good things that normal humans could not do. He stands against evil. He helps people in trouble. He does, in a way, what

God means for Christians to be doing with the supernatural powers he has given to us.

Check out Ephesians 2:10: "For we are God's workmanship, created in Christ Jesus to do good works, which God prepared in advance for us to do." God didn't just save you to get you into heaven with him; He also planned a mission for you—and gave you the supernatural power to pull it off.

Where does all this power come from? Not a toughie. It comes from the only real source of power in the universe—God. Specifically, we get our power from a spirit that comes to live with us at the moment we enter God's family. Called the Holy Spirit, it's actually one part of the trinity that is God.

Okay, what powers are we talking about, exactly?

The Power Not to Sin

Sin is a word that stirs up a lot of ideas and even feelings of guilt. But it really just means "choosing my way over God's way." So sin includes telling a lie, disobeying parents, and anything else a person does that's different from what God would want for us.

When we were still zombies—spiritually dead—*all* we could do was sin. We couldn't *not* sin, because sin was our master. It was what drove us to keep going. We were slaves. Sin owned us. But when God makes a person alive at the time that person trusts Christ, that former slave of sin becomes free to serve God.

Listen to what Paul said: "But thanks be to God that, though you used to be slaves to sin...You have been set free from sin and have become slaves to righteousness." (Romans 6:17-18)

Now you can choose whether to sin or not, because you're alive in Christ. That might not sound like a supernatural power, but it's a doozy. Some translations of the Bible use the word *regeneration*, an instant change that God's Spirit does in us when we trust in Christ (Titus 3:5).

Maybe you're thinking, "Wait a minute. I still sin; maybe I'm not saved." But that's not it at all. What God gave you was the *power* to avoid sinning. The problem is that we still have the desire to sin sometimes. We know it's wrong, but we still want it. The point is that we never, ever *have* to give in to the urge to sin. We're free to tell ourselves no.

Believe it or not, that's supernatural power.

The Ability to Become like Jesus

Again, maybe that doesn't sound supernatural to you, but there's nothing more supernatural in the entire universe that turning a dead mortal into a living spiritual being who is becoming more and more perfect every day.

Yes, we still like sin too much. We still do wrong. But not only have we been given the power to turn sin down any time we choose to, we're being made new. God is changing us from the inside out to be like Jesus.

We're not the same: "You have taken off your old self with its practices and have put on the new self, which is being renewed in knowledge in the image of its Creator" (Colossians 3:10).

As you supernaturally become like Jesus, you're going to discover in yourself the growing power to not *want* sin. Instead, you'll be more and more like the Creator—wanting things that lead to life, not things that lead to death and destruction. Again, that's real power.

The Power to Communicate with God

Zombies don't communicate so well. Living spirits—even human ones—have the supernatural ability to talk to and hear from the Living God.

Not only have you now been granted the right to approach God boldly in prayer through Jesus (Hebrews 4:16), the Holy Spirit who lives with you communicates exactly what you mean to God even when you don't know what to say (Romans 8:26).

Without Christ, the living dead don't have that power. It's supernatural. They also don't have the power to clearly hear from God through his Word, because Satan blinds their minds (2 Corinthians 4:4). As a Christian, you have the power to know God through his Word, the Bible. Beyond that, the Holy Spirit gives us even more power to understand God's Word by guiding us into all truth (John 16:13).

This ability to communicate with the God who loves us, created us, and saved us is a supernatural power that far too many of us Christians take for granted. We've heard the words "read your Bible and pray" so much that many of us have just stopped doing it. I guess we think it's too simple to be a real solution.

But knowing God through prayer and Bible study is a special power that gives us even greater power to live for him. Our not taking advantage of that power is like Superman deciding to walk around the world when he could fly it in just a few minutes.

It's a waste of power.

Power Just for You

We could fill this whole book with supernatural powers given to Christians for completing God's mission for us on earth. But we'll end this chapter by talking about supernatural power that God gives specifically to you.

At the moment of salvation—when a zombie becomes alive for the first time and is given the Holy Spirit—each person receives one or more supernatural gifts from the Spirit to do God's work on earth (1 Corinthians 12:11). These spiritual gifts are supernatural abilities to do some specific thing to serve other Christians. The gifts include teaching, encouraging, giving, faith, and many others. You can find lists of the gifts in four main passages: 1 Corinthians 12; Romans 12; Ephesians 4; and 1 Peter 4.

Someone with the gift of encouraging, for example, would have a supernatural ability—above what even other Christians could do—to give encouragement to others. A supernaturally gifted evangelist would have the power to lead unsaved people to make the choice to trust in Christ.

No one person gets all of the gifts, and we don't all get the same gifts. But we all have the same mission: use your supernatural power to serve others (1 Peter 4:10). Don't walk when you can fly. Don't sit when you have the power to serve.

Why does it matter so much? Because we live in a world full of supernatural beings called people. And God loves those beings. He wants his children to serve each other. And he wants us to reach out to the world with the message of Jesus, because he

118

knows that every person will eventually spend forever in one of two very real supernatural locations.

CHAPTER 11: HELL IS...HELL

Maybe the biggest supernatural question of them all is, "What happens to us after we die?" Obviously, it's a tough one to answer, because we don't get many reliable visitors coming back to fill us in on all the details. If we did, Larry King could have them on his show to describe what went on there. Then we'd all know.

That's part of the reason so many people are fascinated with ghosts and psychics. In a sense, they're wishing for clues about life after death. As Christians, we believe they're looking in the wrong places. They're going to a bad source for info on the biggest question of all time.

Of course, people who don't believe in any kind of supernatural world at all aren't really worried about it (too much). If they're right, physical death is followed by...nothing. The heart stops beating, the mind stops thinking, and the person is just gone. The dead body slowly decays and becomes part of the earth once more. Ah, the circle of life.

Surprisingly, only 5 percent of the teenagers in our survey believed that death was the final stop for us. I think that's because God has built into all of us a deep awareness that we are spiritual, as well as physical, that there's more to this life than what we can see and hear and feel. Even many atheists, agnostics, and naturalists simply cannot accept the idea that there's nothing "out there" after we die.

One indication of the growing influence of both ancient Eastern religions and the modern "new age movement" is the fact that 18 percent of the teenagers in our survey said they believe in reincarnation. Unable to accept that death is the end—and unwilling to believe in the reality of a biblical God—they've found a spiritual idea they can live with: A person's soul or spirit returns to earth—and life—as another living thing. We just go round and round and round. It's not surprising that this idea is catching on, because it shows up as one of the most common "answers" to life's biggest question on TV shows, movies, and in music.

Still, a full 60 percent of teenagers agree with the biblical idea that life on this planet is followed by facing God's judgment

What do you believe happens after death?

WHAT YOUR FRIENDS BELIEVE

60%	People face judgment before God for their decisions on earth
18%	A person's spirit is reincarnated and comes back to earth in another form
5%	A person just ceases to exist
17%	Other belief/don't know

for our actions on earth. Not all agreed on how God would make that judgment, of course. Christians believe the Bible teaches that our souls face one of two supernatural destinations for all time—everlasting torment in hell or a perfect future with God in heaven.

And although we're talking about the supernatural, we'll see that the Bible pictures heaven and hell as entirely real and physical places—not just spiritual "experiences." Both exist in a physical way that can be touched, smelled, seen, and heard.

Hell

Of course, most people don't like to talk about hell. I sure don't. I'd much rather skip the whole subject, because it's painful and stirs up lots of negative emotions. It's just terrible to think about.

In his book *The Problem of Pain*, C.S. Lewis said this about hell: "There is no doctrine I would more willingly move from Christianity than this, if it lay...in my power. I would pay any price to be able to say truthfully, 'All will be saved.' "

I know exactly how he feels. Including a belief in hell makes Christianity much harder to accept. So much harder, in fact, that while 61 percent of the teenagers in our survey believe in a real heaven, only 44 percent believe in a real hell. The idea of everlasting punishment is so uncomfortable that 17 percent of heaven-believers just flat-out refuse to accept it.

You might not guess this from the media, but almost every major religion (not just Christianity) includes teaching on punishment in the afterlife (or the next life) for those who do evil. But all of those religions (and, sadly, many Christian

What do you believe about hell?

> **WHAT YOUR FRIENDS BELIEVE**

44%	A real place of physical torment where people may be sent after death
25%	Not a real place, but a state of permanent separation from God's presence
17%	Not a physical place or a state of being; just a symbolic term
9%	Not a place, but a reference to the fact that people cease to exist after death
5%	Other/don't know

teachers) have toned down their discussions of hell and punishment in recent years. It's just too unpopular.

I've even heard some Christians say, "I'm just into Jesus, man. He's all about love and kindness and forgiveness. I'm not into that Old Testament God of vengeance." Apparently, these folks haven't actually read much of what Jesus is quoted as saying in the New Testament. Lots of what we know about hell came straight from the lips of Jesus.

In fact, Jesus talked about hell more than any other person in the Bible. According to John Blanchard's book *What Ever Happened to Hell?*, 13 percent of the 1,870 verses that include Jesus' words deal with judgment and hell. More than half of Jesus'

40 parables talk about God's eternal judgment of sinners. And 11 of the 12 mentions of the strongest word for hell in the New Testament came from him.

Why did Jesus talk with so much passion and forcefulness about such an ugly topic? Because as God, he knew how real and painful hell really is. No one else who has ever walked the earth was as aware of the torturous reality of hell as Jesus was. And because he is loving and compassionate, he desperately wanted to warn people so they would do what it takes to avoid ever experiencing hell for themselves.

"But wait a minute," I hear someone saying. "Jesus didn't come to condemn the world. That's in the Bible." And that's exactly right. The verses following the most famous verse of all time make it clear that he didn't come the first time he was here to judge—He came to offer every person a way to avoid judgment. He came to show us how *not to go to hell:*

> For God so loved the world that he gave his one and only Son, that whoever believes in him shall not perish but have eternal life. For God did not send his Son into the world to condemn the world, but to save the world through him. Whoever believes in him is not condemned, but whoever does not believe stands condemned already because he has not believed in the name of God's one and only Son. This is the verdict: Light has come into the world, but men loved darkness instead of light because their deeds were evil. Everyone who does evil hates the light, and will not come into the light for fear that his deeds will be exposed. (John 3:16-20)

The bottom line from Jesus is this: Those who reject

him as their only hope for being in heaven will go to hell. Period. There is no heaven without Jesus. So what can they expect when they get there?

Meaninglessness

The strongest word Jesus used for hell was *Gehenna*. The people of his time knew it as the Valley of Ben Hinnom, not far from Jerusalem. They knew that people had once sacrificed their children to false gods there. An evil king of Israel used the place for demonic experiments; he "practiced sorcery, divination and witchcraft, and consulted mediums and spiritists" (2 Chronicles 33:6). We know from the prophet Jeremiah that it was a place of mass graves (Jeremiah 7:32).

125

However, Jesus wasn't saying this physical place on earth was hell itself. He was using the word to describe what hell is like. By his time, it had become a constantly burning landfill of garbage—the city dump.

Thus, the picture of hell we get is one of burning, stench, worms, and—above all—a place where useless things are cast away into a meaningless existence.

Fire, Darkness, Suffering

It's common to hear things like, "I'd rather go to hell and party with my friends than go to heaven and have to play harps and be good all the time." People who say this picture hell as a place that might be uncomfortable, but at least you can be with people you like. What an ignorant concept.

The Bible never describes anything that would make us think of hell as a community of souls. Instead, it's pictured as a place of utter despair:

> Then death and Hades were thrown into the lake of fire. The lake of fire is the second death. If anyone's name was not found written in the book of life, he was thrown into the lake of fire. (Revelation 20:14-15)

> But the subjects of the kingdom will be thrown outside, into the darkness, where there will be weeping and gnashing of teeth. (Matthew 8:12)

126

> Do not be afraid of those who kill the body but cannot kill the soul. Rather, be afraid of the One who can destroy both soul and body in hell. (Matthew 10:28)

Eternal fire. Total, pitch-black darkness. Endless torment and suffering right alongside Satan and the other demons (Revelation 14:11; 20:10). Doesn't leave room for much partying—or hope.

Prison

My best friend once worked at a jail in South Central Los Angeles. I remember touring the place and feeling overwhelmed by the sight of people caged up in small places like animals. But those guys had it pretty good compared to prisoners in Jesus' day.

Then, you could be thrown in prison for having an unpaid debt. While in prison, you weren't guaranteed food or medical treatment, unless someone on the outside agreed to bring it to you. And you weren't released unless you paid back the debt.

If you couldn't pay it, you never got out.

Jesus described hell this way in a parable (Matthew 18:21-35). A man who owed the king more than he could ever pay (and who responded in an evil way to the king's offer to forgive the debt) was sent to prison essentially forever.

Hell is an everlasting prison for those who have rejected God's offer of forgiveness through Jesus.

Separation from God

The absolute worst thing about hell will be existing for eternity without God. Those who reject him by rejecting Jesus will get exactly what they've asked for—the complete absence of him forever:

127

> He will punish those who do not know God and do not obey the gospel of our Lord Jesus. They will be punished with everlasting destruction and shut out from the presence of the Lord and from the majesty of his power. (2 Thessalonians 1:8-9)

Even for unbelievers, the presence of God in our world (and in Christians) makes life worth living. Where does love come from? Truth? Order? Meaning? All from God. Without him, all that will be left is hate, lies, chaos, futility.

As his creation, we were designed to be with God. Even Christians carry an emptiness because we are still physically separated from him. To be completely cut off from him forever will be endless agony.

Why?

Of course, this description of hell from the Bible raises a valid question. What kind of loving God would send anyone there? How *could* he?

First, he doesn't want to do it: " 'Do I take any pleasure in the death of the wicked?' declares the Sovereign LORD. 'Rather, am I not pleased when they turn from their ways and live?' " (Ezekiel 18:23)

God is not cruel. He doesn't delight in the suffering of his creation. He'd rather that nobody ever die and be separated from himself (2 Peter 3:9). So why would he send anyone to hell?

Because he must. God cannot allow sin to go unpunished. He can't live with it—which is what heaven is, living with God.

Imagine if we were at a hospital together, visiting sick people. After a while, you tell me you're thirsty and want a drink. I look around and find a fountain for water and some ice, but I can't locate a cup to bring it to you.

However, when I duck into a supply closet in the infectious diseases wing of the hospital, I find a bedpan. *That'll work,* I think. But when I go to pick it up, I realize it's full of the worst stuff you can imagine. And it's been there for a while. And it reeks. And it's slopping over the edges.

Eventually, you come and find me. You see me put on rubber gloves and dump out the bed pan—and the smell makes you gag. You watch me rinse it out and wipe it off. You then look on as I fill it with ice and water and bring it to you to drink.

How much do you want? If you're smart, you won't take a drop. Even if the water looks okay, all we'd have to do is take it to the lab and use the microscope to see the particles of waste and disease in there.

When we suggest that God should welcome sin (basically, any rejections of him) into heaven, that's far, far worse than drinking that foul, disgusting stuff. Sin repulses him. It's against his nature. He cannot—and will not—live with it.

He knows we're all sinners (Romans 3:23). That's why he made a way for us to miss hell by having our sins forgiven through Jesus. Listen to how the New Living Translation of Romans 5:8-11 describes what God did to save us and brings us home with him:

> But God showed his great love for us by sending Christ to die for us while we were still sinners. And since we have been made right in God's sight by the blood of Christ, he will certainly save us from God's judgment. For since we were restored to friendship with God by the death of his Son while we were still his enemies, we will certainly be delivered from eternal punishment by his life. So now we can rejoice in our wonderful new relationship with God—all because of what our Lord Jesus Christ has done for us in making us friends of God.

God's Word is clear. Nobody has to go to hell. We have a choice. Next, let's look at where we can expect to live forever if we trust in Jesus for our salvation from that terrible, horrible place.

CHAPTER 12: HOME

Almost every religion on earth includes the idea of heaven. Even most people who don't consider themselves religious at least *like* the concept. They hope it's true. They tell their kids that "Grammy is in heaven now," even if they can't say with complete certainty that there is such a place.

For Bible-believing Christians, that hope in a real and supernatural heaven isn't just a great big wish. It's not a cross-our-fingers-and-blow-out-the-candles kind of hope. It's a solid hope. A real hope. It's a hope based on believing that God does not lie.

Listen to the writer of Hebrews: "Now faith is being sure of what we hope for and certain of what we do not see" (11:1). I've never seen a snapshot of the golden streets of heaven. I can't find a downloadable QuickTime movie of heaven anywhere on the Internet. No live Webcams capture the massive pearly gates.

But I know it's there. It's everything I'm hoping for. It's the promise of God that means the most to me. Why? Heaven is my home.

What do you believe about heaven?

WHAT YOUR FRIENDS BELIEVE

61%   Heaven is a real place or paradise where people can go when they die

22%   Heaven is not a place, but it represents a state of connection with the presence of God

13%   Heaven is not real place, but a symbolic term

4%   Other/don't know

131

Of course, people who can't bring themselves to trust a God they cannot see aren't so sure. In our survey of American teenagers, 22 percent said heaven is not a real place at all—just a connection to God's presence. Another 13 percent can only accept the idea of heaven as a hopeful symbol of a peaceful afterlife.

Movies, TV shows, and pop songs offer more confusion about heaven. An '80s pop hit said that "heaven is a place on earth" when you're in love with the right person. On *Buffy the Vampire Slayer*, Buffy actually died and went to heaven, then came back and realized how dark the world is by comparison.

In a book called *What Dreams May Come* by Richard Matheson—and a Robin Williams movie based on it—heaven is pictured with great imagination as a place of vibrant color and wonder, specifically tailored to each individual's idea of greatest happiness. On the flip side, it's also seen as a place of potential loneliness and, strangely, godlessness.

Countless other films (apparently with smaller budgets) reveal heaven as mostly white light, with rolling clouds, and aggravatingly unhelpful angles or formerly living humans. It's also seen as the staging area between reincarnated lives.

Let's wrap up our look at the world of the supernatural by digging out a little of what the Bible says about a very real place called heaven.

Resurrection Bodies

Some of our first clues about the experience of heaven come from the night Jesus was killed and the days that followed. A ton of supernatural events happened in those few days to show God's amazing power over death. It must have been a spooky few days in Jerusalem.

A couple of the weirdest things happened at the moment Jesus' died. First, "the curtain of the temple was torn in two from top to bottom" (Matthew 27:51). This curtain was huge and thick and it separated the "presence of God" in the temple from the area where people were allowed to be.

This supernatural event showed that at the minute of Jesus' death, the separation between humans and God was over. Anyone who trusts in Jesus can now approach God and will ultimately be in heaven with him.

What happened next is even weirder: "The tombs broke open and the bodies of many holy people who had died were raised to life" (27:52). Dead people who had lived their lives in a way that honored God came back to life! They were resurrected the moment Jesus gave up his spirit.

How creepy would it be to see Uncle Lou walk into your house years after his funeral? We're not sure what happened to these people. It's likely that they died again or were taken to heaven. But the fact that God brought them back at the moment of Jesus' death proved that God has conquered death once and for all. Now it is possible for people to live in heaven with him forever.

We learn most about the experience of heaven from Jesus' resurrection. His body was glorified once he came back from the dead. For at least 40 days, he was in his resurrection body on earth—able to appear, disappear, and walk through solid objects, recognizable to those who knew him, able to eat but not needing to do so.

133

Why does that matter to us? Because we, too, will be resurrected. Yes, most of us will die a physical death before the end of the world—but Christians will be raised again just as Jesus was (John 5:28-29). We will have physical bodies again, but they won't be the same as we remember them.

Paul wrote this about our made-for-heaven bodies: "Now we know that if the earthly tent [our body] we live in is destroyed, we have a building from God [a new body], an eternal house in heaven, not built by human hands. Meanwhile we groan, longing to be clothed with our heavenly dwelling" (2 Corinthians 5:1-2).

A Place for Us

Our next clue about heaven comes from something Jesus said to his disciples about his return to heaven after his death and resurrection. They didn't really understand everything he was telling them, but they were understandably freaked out about the idea of losing Jesus.

He told them: "Do not let your hearts be troubled. Trust in God; trust also in me. In my Father's house are many rooms; if it were not so, I would have told you. I am going there to prepare a place for you. And if I go and prepare a place for you, I will come back and take you to be with me that you also may be where I am" (John 14:1-3).

Jesus went to prepare a place for them—and for us! The idea seems to be that every child in the family of God will be given a room—a place—just for us in the Father's house. It will be our home with our huge family forever and ever. It's a place where we will belong and where we'll be loved, cared for, and included.

And what a place it will be! Most of what we know about this home in the afterlife is from the Book of Revelation. Its author, John, was one of Jesus' disciples and closest companions during Jesus' three years on earth. He called himself "the disciple Jesus loved."

Late in his life, John was given a supernatural vision of heaven. In this vision, he was taken to heaven by an angel to see what it was like so he could write it all down. Here are just a few of the things we know about heaven from John's description in Revelation 21:

• Heaven's greatest city is called the new Jerusalem, and it is a huge cube. Unbelievably, it is 1,400 miles wide, long, and high. That means each side is the distance from Arizona to Georgia!

• The walls of the city are made of a brilliant blue gem called jasper, and they're 216 feet thick. The city itself, including the streets, is made of transparent gold.

• Each of the 12 gates into the city—three per side—is made of a single, massive pearl and is guarded by an angel. They stand open all the time. On each gate is written one of the names of the 12 tribes of Israel.

• The city is built on 12 massive foundation stones made of 12 separate precious gems. On each stone is written the name of one of the twelve apostles.

• It is never night. The glory of God fills the whole city, meaning there's no need for any other light source. No sun. No moon. And also no temple or church. The inhabitants of the city are in God's presence all the time, so they never need to gather in one place to worship him.

• Heaven will tower above the new earth (also part of the afterlife), and it will be free of any kind of sin or wickedness or evil. There will be nothing to fear from anyone.

The Best Part

Absolutely the best part of John's vision of heaven is...well, let's let him tell it:

> And I heard a loud voice from the throne saying, "Now the dwelling of God is with men, and he will live with them. They will be his people, and God himself will be with them and be their God." (Revelation 21:3)

God with us! That's what it's all about. The whole story of human history leads up to this moment. Every human heart longs to be with God—because that's what we were created for. That's what we lost when Adam and Eve bought the lie of the serpent and disobeyed God. That's what we'll regain finally and forever in heaven.

What will that change mean for us personally?

He will wipe every tear from their eyes. There will be no more death or mourning or crying or pain, for the old order of things has passed away. (21:4)

What's the reason for all the pain in our earth-bound, painful, human lives? Yes, it's sin, but it's more than that. It's being away from God. Paul wrote this about painful life on planet earth, even for Christians:

We know that the whole creation has been groaning as in the pains of childbirth right up to the present time. Not only so, but we ourselves, who have the firstfruits of the Spirit, groan inwardly as we wait eagerly for our adoption as sons, the redemption of our bodies. (Romans 8:22-23)

The pain we all carry through this life will vanish in the presence of our God. With new bodies and a "new order" of living with him, the separation at long last will end forever. No crying. No pain. No tears. No illness. No death.

Finally, we'll be reunited with all those we love who have died. And those who lost us to death will be with us again, too. The family will be complete, and we'll be together forever with no anger or fear and worry. We'll be with the Father.

Know Hope

In the meantime, how should we live in this natural world? What should believers do with all this knowledge of our supernatural selves, our supernatural enemy, and the supernatural future awaiting us in heaven?

I'm convinced that when it comes to the world of the supernatural, the most important things are what you do with your mind—and your heart. Let's let Paul teach the final lesson on how Christians should live in an age fascinated with the supernatural.

Remember That You Belong to God

Colossians 3 starts with these words, "Since, then, you have been raised with Christ..."

The supernatural world can be scary and confusing. Hopefully, you've gained the tools in this book to better spot the lies and hoaxes about spiritual things. I also hope you've learned what it takes to protect yourself from real supernatural evil.

But the most important thing to remember is that you belong to God. God's Word teaches that when we trust in Christ for our salvation we die with him, in a way. We die to our way of living and become alive to his way of living.

That means we belong to God forever and ever. Nothing can change that for a Christian. Even when other ideas scare you or tempt you, you are still God's. Don't forget that.

Set Your Heart on Heaven

Colossians 3 continues: "Since, then, you have been raised with Christ, set your hearts on things above, where Christ is seated at the right hand of God" (3:1).

Never forget that you're a supernatural being with an everlasting future in heaven. The saddest thing in the world is when Christians (including myself) find more joy and excitement from the temporary things of the world than we do from our future with the Father.

138   In his book, *The Weight of Glory*, C.S. Lewis compared us to kids playing in mud puddles in the back yard. Even when given a chance to go to the beach and play in the ocean, we don't stop, because we can't image what the beach will be like. We love the mud, because it's all we know.

Part of becoming a mature spiritual person is learning that nothing on this earth can satisfy us for long. Our only hope of real satisfaction and meaning comes at the end of the story, when we'll be reunited with God and our loved ones forever.

My friend Bart from Mercy Me was thinking of his grandfather when he wrote the now widely-loved song, "I Can Only Imagine." He nailed this point. Setting our hearts on heaven means taking the time to imagine what being in the presence of God together will be like. That song helps me to live in the hope of heaven.

Think about Heavenly Things

"Since, then, you have been raised with Christ, set your hearts on things above, where Christ is seated at the right hand of God. Set your minds on things above, not on earthly things" (Colossians 3:1-2).

In the end, your interaction with the supernatural world will come down to what you do with your mind. Will you fill it with the supernatural ideas and images of the world? Will you become an expert on *Harry Potter* or *Buffy* or *Star Wars* or *The Matrix*? Will you chase your curiosity into Wiccan teachings or angel worship or flirting with evil?

139

I hope this book has helped you understand the emptiness and danger of making those things the main focus of your life. Again, I'm not teaching that you should never consume any movies, books, or TV shows that address those themes. What I'm asking is: What's the main thing for you?

If the main thing in your life is your relationship with God through Jesus, how much of your time do you spend thinking about heavenly things? How much of God's Word are you putting into your mind and thoughts? How often do you talk to God about stuff?

If you're going to get serious in your supernatural relationship with the ultimate supernatural being, you might have to do something radical. You might have to turn off the TV and the Web and study his Word. On purpose. On a regular basis.

It's the most powerful supernatural experience you can have on earth. And it's very, very real.

The Promise

Paul concludes that paragraph at the beginning of Colossians 3 with a promise: "Your life is now hidden with Christ in God. When Christ, who is your life, appears, then you will appear with him in glory." (3:3-4)

Your real life, your actual home, isn't on this planet, anymore. Not if you're a follower of Jesus. All your supernatural mail is being forwarded to an address in heaven. That's where you live. You're a foreigner here now.

140   Everything in this world will end. The time is coming when Christ will make himself known to everyone, and God's Word will be proved true. Those who now mock your faith in what can't be seen or touched or heard will know then that you were right.

Hold on. Don't give up. Live like a supernatural being who belongs to another time and place. Keep trusting God all the way home.

AFTERWORD: LIVING SUPERNATURALLY

Imagine that you are someone who is fascinated by airplanes. You could spend a lifetime studying how planes work. What principles of physics allow those big metal birds to get off the ground? How much power does it take to get them up there? How high can they go? Which plane builders are the best?

You could know all that stuff about airplanes—without ever knowing how to fly one yourself.

Knowing about planes and knowing how to fly them are two different things. I'm sure that knowing the physics of airplanes would be helpful for flying one, but it doesn't guarantee that you'll be able to land a 747 in the fog, right?

In the same way, knowing about the supernatural world and actually living wisely in it doesn't always go together.

In this book, we've tried to grow in what we know about the supernatural world. We've learned that the Bible is the ultimate source of information about it. We've studied God, angels, Satan, demons, heaven, and hell.

We've talked about ghosts, vampires, talking to the dead, reincarnation, and other ideas that distract people from the truth about the supernatural. We've explored some of the ways people get fooled into believing lies about the world beyond our senses.

But all that "knowing" will be useless if we don't do something with it. Let's spend a couple of pages here at the end of this thing to remember how God tells us to live supernaturally.

1) Fear God, but don't be afraid of him.

God is the ultimate supernatural being. He's the source of everything in the universe—whether we can see it or not. He's an invisible spirit, and he can do anything he wants at any time he wants to anyone he wants. It's his show.

For Christians, living supernaturally always starts with respecting God's power above all. Especially in the Old Testament, the Bible calls that attitude of respect for God "fear."

And if you don't respect God's power at least as much as you respect the power of a hurricane or tornado or nuclear bomb, you don't really get it. He's a million times more powerful than any of those things.

Of course, believers in Jesus don't have to be afraid of God—even while we respect his power. Why? Because that awesome supernatural being has adopted us into his own family through Jesus. We're his kids! Romans 8:15 reads, "For you did not receive a spirit that makes you a slave again to fear, but you received a Spirit of sonship. And by him we cry, 'Abba, Father.' "

Living supernaturally must start with understanding

that the ultimate supernatural power is our Father.

2) Don't seek out a conversation with any supernatural being but God (and other humans).

Angels fascinate us. We learned they were created by God and have lots of incredible powers. God may have even used angels to answer your prayers.

But the Bible warns us not to worship angels. They're not God. And we're never told to talk to them or to try to communicate with them in any way. The Bible warns that Satan masquerades as an angel of light (2 Corinthians 11:14), and in Galatians 1:8 we are cautioned not to listen to an angel who presents a gospel different from what is revealed in Scripture. Any person or book or movie that suggests we can get power or knowledge through reaching out to angels is lying.

143

In the same way, God never tells us to look for ways to communicate with ghosts or dead people. In fact, the Bible sternly warns against this. It's not God's plan for his children to gain knowledge by talking to a loved one (or anyone else) who has died.

That rules out using Ouija boards or psychics or any other kind of mediums to "the other side." They are all either frauds or they're harnessing power that's not from God. For believers, that's the wrong way to live supernaturally.

Finally, God doesn't encourage us to chat with Satan or other demons, either. They're specialty is lying. Even if we succeed in communicating with them somehow, we're setting ourselves up to be deceived.

What if you're being demonically oppressed or fear that Satan is influencing your life? Shouldn't you tell him to get lost, like so many Christian teachers suggest? I don't think so. Who is it that frees you from the power of Satan and demons? God does it through the Holy Spirit in a believer's life. So go to God directly and ask him to take care of the enemy.

Why is this such a big deal? Two reasons. One, God wants us to come to him for information and communication with the supernatural world. That's why he provided his Word and why he made it possible for us to talk to him through prayer.

Second, if you can talk to the most powerful supernatural being in the universe and know that he hears you, why would you need to talk to any other being? God is the only direct contact with the supernatural world that we need.

3) Respect the power of Satan and demons, but don't obsess about them.

As we studied, God urges us to take Satan's supernatural power seriously. He's a roaming lion out to destroy us. He's a liar out to deceive us. Satan and his army of fallen angels are a serious threat.

Living supernaturally means taking that threat seriously. Put on the spiritual armor of Ephesians 6. Ask for God's protection. Take the time to know God's Word well enough that you're not easy to fool when the enemy tries to trip you up.

Mostly, resist this supernatural enemy by getting closer to God. James 3:7-8 promises that Satan will flee when we get closer to God. If the danger is real, don't be afraid to take drastic measures to protect yourself.

What kind of drastic measures? Daily prayer. Memorizing Scripture. Avoiding books, movies, and music for entertainment that lead your thinking and emotions toward darkness instead of light.

On the other hand, our relationship with God is not just about avoiding the enemy. Yes, Satan can trip us up and slow us down—even lead us away from the truth. But he cannot steal us away from God. He can't change God's love for us, and he can't change what the truth is. We are totally secure in God's hands.

So we don't need to make our everyday lives about Satan or demons. We don't need to assume that every secular book, song, or movie about the supernatural world is from Satan or guaranteed to lead us into darkness. Satan has no authority over Christians. He is not our master.

4) Practice prayerful wisdom.

What we need most in a world full of supernatural and spiritual ideas is wisdom—the ability to separate truth from lies. Christians must learn to build strong discernment muscles—or we will get caught by the "thinking traps" that snare so many people.

How can we practice discernment? Listen and understand what is being taught about the supernatural world by friends, teachers, entertainment, or anything else that deals with it. Compare it to what the Bible teaches. Ask God for wisdom, and make some choices. Is this teacher presenting the truth or a clever lie? Should I learn more about this or should I walk away because of where it leads my mind and emotions? Should I challenge what this movie is teaching when talking about it with my friends or should I keep my mouth shut?

Those can be hard choices. But God promises wisdom and discernment to make those tough decisions: "If any of you lacks wisdom, he should ask God, who gives generously to all without finding fault, and it will be given him" (Proverbs 1:5).

5) Live in the Spirit.

It might sound creepy, but if you're a Christian you have a foreign Spirit living with you right now. Of course, it's God's Spirit. And as we studied, his Spirit gives you supernatural powers that are out of this world.

Don't ignore that supernatural power; live in it! Use it for good. As that great spiritual leader and web-slinging crimefighter Peter Parker once said, "With great power comes great responsibility." That's not just true for Spider-Man. Because of the Holy Spirit, *you* can have supernatural joy, peace, patience, self-control, and love. Don't settle for a life without those things.

You can also supernaturally make a difference in your church and the world by using the spiritual gifts the Holy Spirit has brought into your life. You can stop being spooked about the supernatural world and start living in it!

6) Live like heaven and hell are real places.

As Christians, we claim there is an eternal place of torture and separation from God called hell. And we also say that for those who accept Christ, this life is just a brief moment before an eternity in heaven with God. We say we believe those things.

But how would people who really believed such ideas live supernaturally? Wouldn't they be involved in doing whatever they could to persuade friends and family to escape eternal punishment by trusting in Jesus? Wouldn't they spend a lot less time worrying about things in this life that are not going to matter to us one hundred years from now—like movies, hair, clothes, and all the other stuff we spend so much time thinking about? Wouldn't they be investing in things that will still matter in heaven?

How would you live today if you knew that a huge earthquake were going to destroy your city tomorrow? What would you do to warn people? On the other hand, how would you live if you knew you were going to receive a million dollars next week? How much time would you spend worrying about your current bank balance?

How we live says a lot about what we really believe. Do you believe in the supernatural world? If so, don't be satisfied with simple belief. Don't settle for just knowing about spiritual things. Start flying the plane yourself. Start living supernaturally today!

QUESTIONS AND ANSWERS

Are ghosts real?

Ghosts are a big part of the increase of supernatural themes in movies, TV, and books. The most common worldview presented in stories about ghosts is that they are the spirits of people who died with unfinished business left on earth.

So, in *The Sixth Sense,* a little boy sees—and helps—dead people who need to fix something before they can leave to the great beyond. In *Ghost,* a popular movie from the early '90s, Patrick Swayze sticks around to love and protect Demi Moore after he dies. Nicole Kidman's *The Others* shows ghosts who don't realize they're the ones doing the haunting.

In the real world, evidence for ghosts is scarce. People who take them seriously talk about psychic energy and show photographs with strange lights or colors. But most of the real research suggests that living people tend to create ghosts, either out of fear, grief, or for profit.

For instance, the strangest ghost stories are rarely told by the people who believe they've experienced an encounter with a ghost—unless those people are getting paid. The tellers are almost always people who heard it secondhand.

In addition, people who claim to hear voices or see dead relatives almost always stop experiencing those things when they take antipsychotic medications. That suggests either that ghosts don't like medication or that people who are having intense emotional and psychological problems are more likely to see things that aren't there.

The Bible leaves little room for the existence of ghosts. It never, ever talks about the spirits of dead humans lingering here. Paul wrote that for Christians, to be away from the body is to be present with God (2 Corinthians 5:8). And the Bible describes very specific judgments for unbelievers—judgments that do not include becoming a haunting spirit on earth (2 Thessalonians 1:9).

What's up with vampires and werewolves?

Our current ideas about supernatural creatures called vampires and werewolves come primarily from entertainment sources: the original *Dracula* movies of the 1930s and dozens of sequels and adaptations since then; the books of Anne Rice; and the world created by the popular shows *Buffy the Vampire Slayer* and *Angel*.

According to the myth, a vampire is a demon who inhabits the body of a human. They need to drink blood to stay alive; they're very strong; they can live forever; but they can be killed by sunlight, a stake through the heart, or being exposed to religious symbols like crosses or holy water. Oh, and they can turn other people into vampires if they want.

Werewolves are mythical creatures that appear human during the day, yet turn into ferocious and dangerous wolves when the moon is full. A person bitten by a werewolf will become one, and then he or she can only be killed while a wolf by a silver bullet. (They hate garlic, too.)

It's possible that these monsters of movies, TV, and books got their start in the real world. According to a great book by James Watkins called *Death and Beyond* (Tyndale, 1993), researchers at the University of British Columbia have studied a rare disease called *porphyria*. Victims of this illness can't produce *heme*, the red pigment in the blood's hemoglobin.

They believe some early sufferers tried to alleviate their symptoms by drinking blood. In addition, without that substance in their blood, these people are painfully sensitive to light. Sunlight causes sores that deform their hands; the skin of the face gets thin and tight, causing the teeth to stick out. And the body tries to protect itself with increased (wolf-like?) hair growth.

Finally, people with this disease are also violently allergic to garlic. It's possible that the legends grew out of a real-world illness.

The Bible, of course, teaches that demons are very real and that they can, in fact, possess unbelievers, making them violent and giving them supernatural strength. However, the Bible doesn't ever talk about these people living unnaturally long lives.

Are there any real psychics?

As explored elsewhere in this book, illusionists and "psychic entertainers" who pretend to have psychic power are highly trained and skilled professionals. They are excellent at getting people to reveal information about themselves, and then feeding that information back in ways that are convincing.

I've seen it done over and over again. In fact, I've done similar tricks before thousands of people. None of the supposed psychics I've met had any real power. In fact, most freely admit (when not performing) that they're just really good at fooling people.

There's no real-world evidence or biblical suggestion that any human being naturally possesses the power to read minds, move objects with his mind, or talk to the dead. However, there's a trickier question: Is it possible for Satan or a demon to deliver information through a person that he or she couldn't otherwise know?

The Bible says yes. On at least two occasions, people who would not have otherwise recognized Jesus as the Son of God knew who he was because they were demon-possessed. So it's at least possible that a psychic, medium, or spiritist could get info supernaturally from a demon. But such occurrences are uncommon, even in the Bible.

If that did happen, would the information be reliable? Remember the devil's native language? Lying. Deception. That's what demons do.

So if you encounter a psychic, it's most likely that this person is a fraud or an "entertainer." There's a much smaller possibility that a demon may be using this psychic to deceive and tell lies. Either way, there's no reason to trust psychics or the information they give you.

Is it possible to speak to the dead?

Even if a psychic or medium were empowered by Satan or a demon, could this person actually contact spirits of the dead and tell you what they wanted to say to you?

Of course, if a supposed psychic could convince you he had contact with a dead relative, he could say that spirit was telling you something, and there would be no way to verify it. But you could ask him to have the spirit describe something only that person who has died (and you) would know.

152   Using that standard, no psychic has ever proved his ability to talk to the dead. Usually, what they'll say is, "Oh, it doesn't work that way."

James Randi is a well-known magician and escape artist who has dedicated his life to scientifically dismantling false claims about the supernatural world. He is not friendly to Christianity, either, since he believes the Bible is unsupportable. However, his foundation has done a lot to expose psychics and those who claim to talk to spirits.

For decades, his foundation has had a standing offer to anyone who could demonstrate any supernatural power. If a psychic can verifiably prove a paranormal event, Randi says he will give that person $1 million. To date, no psychic has passed even the preliminary tests to make a claim for the prize. If psychics really can talk to the dead, doesn't it make sense that someone could easily prove it and claim the prize?

Elsewhere in this book, we explore one biblical account where a king of Israel used a psychic to call up the spirit of a dead prophet (1 Samuel 28). As stated there, this was likely a supernatural act of God—not any work of a psychic with supernatural power or a demon.

How do astrology and horoscopes work?

Those who believe in astrology teach that both your personality and the events of your life are determined, to some extent, by the time of year that you were born. Each of the 12 signs of the zodiac calendar—Capricorn, Pisces, etc.—is assigned to a range of dates.

A horoscope is a prediction or evaluation of what a day, month, or year will be like for persons based on their sign of the zodiac. Writers of horoscopes are very skilled at crafting careful paragraphs that contain several elements that could apply to nearly anyone.

153

For example, here's a horoscope I found online: "Today you could well want to set aside a block of time to spend with close friends, or with a love partner. Other responsibilities, however, could have you out and about on your own, taking care of errands and other important matters. At some point you may have the feeling of being 'lonely in a crowd.' Don't waste time feeling sorry for yourself. Take care of business and then get back to your loved ones."

If I believed in horoscopes, I might try to live by the predictions and directions in this. But a careful reading shows two things.

1) This could apply to anyone. Who wouldn't benefit from spending time with loved ones? Who doesn't sometimes have to

do things on his or her own? Shouldn't everyone reject self-pity, get their business done, and get back to people they care about?

2) If I read this early in my day, I'm likely to be aware of it all day. It works as a self-fulfilling prophecy. Any time I spend with loved ones—or alone—is likely to confirm my idea that the person who wrote this has some supernatural knowledge of people based on their dates of birth.

So are horoscopes harmless? No. For one, they can warp your thinking about what really matters; following them can lead you away from what you should really be doing with your life. Two, God wants his followers to rely on him for direction and wisdom.

Exposing ourselves to false teachers (2 Peter 2:1) opens us up to being deceived about the truth—and being influenced by liars, including supernatural liars.

Do people come back in another form after they die?

Reincarnation is a major belief of those who follow the New Age movement, as well as several ancient Eastern religions. It has gained popularity in America recently, and is showing up in many movies, TV shows, and books.

The Bible flatly contradicts the idea that a person can come back for multiple lives: "Just as man is destined to die once, and after that to face judgment, so Christ was sacrificed once to take away the sins of many people" (Hebrews 9:27-28).

We humans die only one physical death, then we face

God's judgment. That closes the door on multiple lives for those who believe the Bible. This life is the only opportunity we get to respond to God's offer of the free gift of salvation through Jesus.

How do Magic 8 Balls, Ouija boards, and Tarot cards work?

The Magic 8 Ball, of course, is sold in toy stores. It's a sphere made to look like a billiard ball. It works like rolling a die, except that you shake it and the "die" floats to the top of the liquid inside so you can see what it says through a little window.

When you ask it questions and shake it, you get answers like "Yes," "No," and "I Don't Know." You could play the game without an 8 Ball by assigning the same answers to regular dice numbers and rolling them.

155

A Ouija ("wee-gee") board is a "game" in which you also ask a question. You then determine the answer by having two people hold a pointer at the same time and allowing themselves to be "directed" in their movements around an alphabet on the board to spell out answers.

Tarot cards are like large playing cards with certain images printed on them. Usually used by a psychic or fortune-teller, they supposedly tell the future of a person being "read." These are also easy to get in novelty shops or on the Internet.

None of these devices has any supernatural power on its own. None of them is known to work any more accurately than flipping a coin. Consulting them for information about our lives or our future is just as futile and dangerous as going to a psychic or reading horoscopes.

When we look for real, supernatural information from sources other than God, Satan and his demons can use those things to deceive us. I'm not saying that spirits actually make the 8 Ball answer a certain way, take over the pointer on a Ouija board, or direct which cards come up in a deck of Tarot. (Although, it's possible for a demon to control a person using the tools.)

What I am saying is that the very act of looking to those things for guidance shows that we're not relying on God. And if we do it for real, we're asking "other spirits" to guide our lives. That's dangerous territory.

156 Can anyone really predict the future?

The Bible is full of stories about persons God used to predict the future. They were called prophets, and almost all of them worked and lived in Old Testament times. Thus, we know that God can supernaturally empower people to predict the future.

Does God still work that way today? For the most part, no. Christians believe that God's Word is his complete message to us. He no longer needs prophets to communicate to us what he's thinking. However, that doesn't mean he couldn't do that.

So how would you know if a message about the future was from God or not? For one, according to the rules for prophets in the Old Testament, the person making the prediction would have to be 100 percent right about their predictions all the time. God told the Israelites to put to death any prophet who claimed to speak for God if his predictions didn't come true (Deuteronomy 18:20-22).

The other important thing about prophets of God is that

they will never proclaim anything that contradicts God's Word, the Bible. If they do, they are false prophets.

How about on the other side? Can Satan or demons work through people to make predictions about the future? Nothing in the Bible indicates that Satan or demons know specific things about the future (other than their own fate). But even if they did, we must keep in mind what Satan's goal is. To deceive. To lie. To mislead.

Therefore, any prediction made by anyone other than a prophet of God isn't worth hearing. Again, it's either a hoax or a supernatural message designed to trip us up. There's no good reason to look for predictions of the future aside from the Bible.

Do magicians like David Copperfield and David Blaine have any real power?

Nope. Well, they have the power to get specials on TV, but that's about it. I've actually hired some of the people who work with David Copperfield to help me come up with illusions for my performances. They're great at tricking people.

It's easy to get spooked when we "see" David Blaine levitate in broad daylight or Copperfield make the Statue of Liberty disappear. But it's all just trickery.

What is Wicca?

Wicca is a nature-based, pagan religion that includes worship of both the earth and gods or goddesses. Among other things, Wiccans believe that the power of the earth can be accessed for good purposes, and that you can get power from supernatural sources.

The religion of Wicca is experiencing rapid growth in American and Canada, especially among teenage girls. Its popularity is evident from browsing the number of books and Web sites available on the topic right now.

Wiccans don't agree with each other in all their beliefs about the supernatural, but many Wiccans also practice witchcraft or magic (sometimes called *magick*). By casting spells or through other means, they seek to control the forces of nature or spirits to do helpful or hurtful things for themselves or other people.

Biblical Christians believe that Wicca is an extremely dangerous religion. Since we understand all spirits other than God (and the angels he controls) to be demonic, our belief is that those who call on spirits to take action in their lives may actually be in contact with demons. And since demons have the power to influence and control unbelievers, Wiccans expose themselves to the control of Satan.

The other problem with Wicca is that in some ways, it is also about rebellion against the God of the Bible. Many Wiccans are attracted to the religion's emphasis on the power of the female and feminism, sexuality (including homosexuality), and rejection of a masculine, all-controlling God. They see traditional Christianity as intolerant.

Are witches real?

Without a doubt, many people see themselves as witches and practice what they call magick or witchcraft. Most do not see themselves as traditional satanists: Either they do not believe in Satan, or they don't worship him. Instead, they see witchcraft as a way of accessing the power of the spirit world and of nature.

The recent surge in media spirituality has included large doses of witches and witchcraft. On TV, *Buffy the Vampire Slayer*'s Willow discovered that she was a powerful and gifted witch and used her powers (mostly) to fight evil. The young and attractive women of *Charmed* are witches with even more impressive supernatural powers.

And, of course, the media phenomenon that is *Harry Potter* has made one particular group of witches and wizards hugely popular with kids, teenagers, and adults alike.

159

What's so wrong with experimenting with supernatural power?

Christians believe there is real danger in Wicca, witchcraft, or any other religion or belief system that includes calling on spirits. Why? Because we understand that supernatural power can come from only two sources—God and Satan.

The Bible is clear that God does not respond to requests for supernatural power except from believers in Jesus for clearly defined purposes. Those looking elsewhere for supernatural power will either find no power at all, or they will find supernatural power from Satan and demons. Those are the only options.

God told the Israelites this about the witchcraft and supernaturalism that was popular in their day: "Let no one be found among you who sacrifices his son or daughter in the fire, who practices divination or sorcery, interprets omens, engages in witchcraft, or casts spells, or who is a medium or spiritist or who consults the dead. Anyone who does these things is detestable to the LORD" (Deuteronomy 18:10-12).

The message to followers of the God of the Bible is crystal: Don't mess with any of it—casting spells, witchcraft, magick, wizardry, psychics, or talking to the dead. God hates that stuff.

What about the *Harry Potter* books and movies and other stories that are set in the world of the supernatural? Are these okay?

If you want to get Christians arguing with each other, bring this question up in youth group or on a Christian message board on the Internet. As believers, we're very divided on this issue. At the risk of making someone angry, here's what I think.

There's no question that Christians must have nothing to do with witchcraft or any other kind of supernatural power that is seeking in the real world. It's evil. It's dangerous. It exposes us to the enemy's lies, as well as his power. It's rebellion against God.

Almost all books, movies, TV shows, and music about the supernatural world present a worldview that is different from what the Bible teaches. The biggest difference is this: We believe supernatural power can only come from the biblical God or from Satan. Any story that shows supernatural power coming form any other source is creating a different worldview.

Yes, that would include Harry Potter, because his power and the power used by evil witches and wizards both seem to come from the earth or some other source. God and Satan are not presented. However, Harry's world isn't the only one with that perspective. The same is true in the *Star Wars* movies, most animated Disney movies (*Snow White, The Little Mermaid,* etc.), *Buffy* on TV, and even *The Lord of the Rings* movies.

So if we shouldn't watch the Potter movies because they picture witchcraft and sorcery, we must throw all the others out, as well. Should that be our blanket policy?

My understanding of Scripture in this case is that becomes an individual choice between you, your parents, and God. Here is my understanding of the guidelines:

1. If you're convinced that consuming these stories is wrong, you shouldn't do it. If you think supernatural evil is too serious an issue to be used in storytelling—even stories picturing good versus evil—don't take them in. Entertainment is not a good reason to violate your conscience. But be careful not to condemn those who disagree.

The Bible is clear that believers have the freedom to decide in their own hearts about some issues. I think that applies, to a point, to the issue of the content of the stories we take in. (Check out 1 Corinthians 8 for some teaching on the topic.)

There are definitely valid arguments on both sides of this issue, but disagreement about reading *Harry Potter* is not a good reason to divide groups of Christians.

2. If you're convinced that it's okay to watch a fictional story that includes witchcraft, because you understand the lie and know God's truth, then enjoy your freedom to do so. However, I'd be careful not give such movies too big a place in your life.

There's a difference between listening to a well-told story that disagrees with your worldview in an attempt to understand what the author has to say—and becoming a fanatic or expert in all things to do with that story. For Christians, God's Word should always be a bigger part of our hearts and minds than any movie, book, or show.

Also, be sensitive to your brothers and sisters who don't agree with you. Avoid condemning them. The apostle Paul said that if doing something you believe is okay causes someone else to do something they believe is wrong, then you should be willing to give it up (1 Corinthians 8:13). Being "right" about *Harry Potter* is not as important as loving each other.

3. If you have the strength of conviction to take in supernatural movies and stories that disagree with the Bible's teaching, you should also have the courage to talk about your worldview with friends and family. Popular movies and books about the supernatural are an excellent opportunity to introduce the topic of your supernatural beliefs with unsaved friends. Show the strength of your convictions in those conversations in a loving way.

In other words, don't miss an opportunity to use *Potter* and *The Matrix* and *The Lord of the Rings* to talk about the real supernatural power of Jesus.